Be Creative and Live Forever

FURTHER TWILIGHT RUMINATIONS

Charles C. Finn

PRAISES FOR BE CREATIVE AND LIVE FOREVER

"Wake up! Pay attention to relationships, memories, the news, the suffering of others, language, trees, birds...Charlie Finn takes up the clarion call of poets through the ages and, in so doing, invites his readers to do likewise. His deceptively simple poems are about more than the minute details of a life. Each is imbued with Finn's breathtakingly expansive and inclusive cosmology. Just as William Blake invited his readers to 'see a world in a grain of sand,' these poems invite the reader to see a universe in the mirror. It is impossible to take in these poems and not be enlarged in your ideas of who you are and what you are about."

—Tony Martin, Retired public school teacher, musician, gardener, author/composer of *A Civics Carol*

"I marvel at Charlie Finn. He seems to embody the essence of Psalm 118: 'This is the day that the Lord has made, let us rejoice and be glad in it.' His short poems capture the musings of a fertile mind—on his mentors, his loves, on science, music, nature, on spirit, on world events, and even, sometimes, on despair. Like the mockingbird (a central image in this book) he pours forth songs that anyone can find delight or solace in. Dip into this book—just a little—and you will find yourself coming back to dip some more!"

—Judy Starr Hopping, —Like her name (her real name!) implies, a wanderer who has always drawn comfort from the richness of Nature and the Mysteries of Space and Time

"Reading Charlie Finn's latest book is to be transported into an elegant series of vignettes, sometimes playful, often profound. Finn grounds the spiritual in the senses, such as using dance imagery to describe the relationship between life and death, or the forest as a model for a welcoming faith community. Finn's influences are clear in his reference to writers who have come before him, sometimes interweaving one writer's thoughts with another, such as in Mary Oliver Saluting Her Brother Walt Whitman. In Remembering Maya [Angelou], Finn shows his appreciation with 'Because she was, we can be better.' His many influences are revealed in Glimpse into My Holy of Holies. Finn has created a fine work of love and joy, that doesn't ignore the difficulties of life but uses them to contrast with the moments of peace and inner light. These lovely, well-crafted sketches of life are meant to be sipped and savored, perhaps with the first morning light or the end of a long day."

—Betsy Proch, Quaker and friend

"Come close listen and take a deep dive into the meaning of the universe with *Be Creative and Live Forever*. Poet Charles Finn invites you to journey into the wonders of our human experiences. Written at twilight these poems, including the haiku, are infused with intelligent insights through keen observation and significant human bonds garnered by a life lived with kindness, empathy, courage and truth. Whatever your loves, your personal successes and your traumas in life, immerse yourself in this volume of poems and find heartfelt emotional calm and enlightenment. Open your heart, listen with your mind, read this book and be creative!"

—Barbara Conklin, A reader

"Whether you are new to the wonder of poetry or an experienced reader, *Be Creative and Live Forever* will speak to you. Charlie Finn draws upon a wealth of literary reading and years of lifelong experiences to open your eyes to the beauty, pain, longing, mystery, and richness of life. He writes caringly and thoughtfully of the birth of a child, the death of a friend, the music of a songbird, the mystery of life. I found myself saying over and over again Yes, I have known that, I have felt that, I have seen that."

—Midge Kirby, Pediatric dietitian and fortunate grandmother of eight

"Charlie Finn explores many topics in his poetry, among them religion, ecology, war, politics and health. He looks at them from a deep mysticism and an intense compassion. And he shares his 'ruminations' with a generosity of spirit."

—Gary Sandman, Artist, Director of the Plowshare Peace Center in Roanoke

"Charlie Finn's poems are friendly offerings and gentle nudges toward kinship and enlightenment. The universe, whether or not given a name like God or Great Mystery, winds and flows through his verses. Honest and beautifully crafted, these verses generously share the wisdom of a lifetime seeker. I am struck by how often he ends his poems with questions that invite soul searching on the part of the reader. Treat yourself in *Be Creative and Live Forever* to true poetry of spirit."

—Meg Huston, Artist

"It is a such a pleasure to have Charlie Finn's new book of ruminations where he shares in a way that feels like a walk home with a close friend. His images, like 'a crack in the voice' and 'looking down at gnarled hands,' speak to me. When reading his poems I find it difficult not to slow down and be open to the memories or musings that are called forward. I was lost for some time, for instance, in wondering what I would say or to whom after reading 'If but a Moment Left to Live.' 'In Death on My Left Shoulder' he reminds me to give my gift while I can, precisely what Charlie is doing in this collection, sharing his gifts while he can! This is a volume to keep beside your bed or favorite reading chair. It invites you to slow down and go deep."

—Jane Hundley, A retiring clinical social worker with fifty years of listening to stories people need to share.

"I have always been inspired, touched and grateful for the beauty and wisdom in Charlie Finn's poetry. I think of his new book as existentialism in its purest form, helping me feel one with what he is saying. His words touch the spiritual essence of humanity."

—Nancy Henley, Roanoke Friend since 2003

"Charlie Finn presents to us a multitude of poems to ponder. The proof is in the poems: read, digest, and be enriched! Thousands of students showed me that if they trusted and opened, creativity would flow. From flowers to faces, from deep down where we're all fire, from gnarled hands digging in the ground, Charlie opens his creativity to spark your awareness that you too are part of the creating universe!"

—Gary R Kirby, PhD, Renaissance Literature, fellow poet and friend of Charlie for sixty-five years

"I am indebted to Charlie for introducing me to the world of poetry, such that it has become a love. I find myself rushing through his poems as with a novel until lines suddenly stop me in my tracks with the recognition of a truth or feeling I immediately relate to but could never have found the words to express even to myself. Readers new to his poetry will find no need to dig for hidden meanings. It is straightforward but penetrating. His unique sensitivity to the world is a God given gift yes, but it is hard-earned due to his listening and observing with ever present pen and pad in hand over the past 50 years! I especially appreciated the sprinkling of references to Teilhard de Chardin, illuminating how our everyday creative acts of love fit into Teilhard's great cosmic vision of a universe still birthing. Bottom line: if you're new to Charlie's poetry, you're in for a treat."

—Art Stouffs of Bethesda MD, Retired, former waterfowl hunter of the Chesapeake Bay and member of The Eastern Shore Metaphysical Society

"While I often find poetry to ramble and wander, Charlie strikes with precision! Let your heart be still and receive his art."

—Theron White, YMCA Pool safety and survival swimming instructor

"Charlie Finn's poems express a daily practice of receiving all that comes into him – from the continually evolving universe, from the songs of birds and forest, from the mystery of love and loss, from the presence of ancestors, from the cherished community of friends, and from the beautiful lives of his wife, children, and grandchildren.

This stream of inspiring poems emerges out of a long life of paying attention to gratitude, love, and wisdom. He invites the reader to experience with him this wondrous place where he lives."

—Mike Heller, Member of the Roanoke Quaker Meeting and Professor of English Emeritus, Roanoke College

"Charlie Finn in his new book of poems is inviting us to slow down and feast on our lives. All he asks is that we bring mind and heart and a readiness to savor. Awed by our beautiful, fragile Earth, Charlie stands for compassion and a justice always tempered with mercy. He stands with those who are struggling and feel powerless. His poems never fail to give me hope, peace of heart, and encouragement to fall back in love with life again. Settle in to his poetry and savor a feast."

—Alison Allsbrook, Clinical social worker, passionate for deep friendships and democracy

"The invite in Charlie Finn's new volume of poems, written in the silence of early mornings in the foothills of the Blue Ridge, is to step outside our individual silos to enter into the observations of another member of our species. See it as a gift of possibility thanks to another's vulnerability, an opportunity to reflect, at one's own pace, on snippets of thought or feeling from Charlie's journey across eight decades. Each snippet reminds us that we need imagination and empathy as much as if not more than we need reason and logic. What I get out of *Be Creative and Live Forever* is an invitation to see that there is no 'other.' Rather, there is only a 'we.'"

—Mike Harmon, Retired chief of litigation for the City of Cincinnati, volunteer at Catholic Worker homeless shelter, lover of the written word, and super fan of nature in all its forms including human beings like his life partner and eight grandchildren

Chapin Keith Publishing
Daleville, VA. 24083
www.Chapinkeith.com

Publisher's Cataloging-in-Publication Data

Names: Finn, Charles C. Finn, author.

Title: Be Creative and Live Forever / Charles C. Finn
Identifiers: LCCN: 2025902125 | ISBN 979-8-9919038-5-1 (Paperback) |
979-8-9919038-6-8 (eBook)

BISAC POETRY / General | POETRY/ American/General

Cover and book design by Asya Blue Design
Front cover: Final sunrise for our 250-year old white oak that we named Gandalf
whose diseased branches posed a threat to passing traffic. Our Pomeranian Buckley
seemed to be joining us in bidding Gandalf adieu. Photo by Charles C. Finn

First Edition

Visit the author's website at https://poetrybycharlescfinn.com/

DEDICATED

~~

To: Loren Eiseley
Sue Monk Kidd
Mary Oliver
Teilhard de Chardin
and E. E. Cummings
whose spirits (along with many others)
infuse these pages

We forget that nature itself is one vast miracle transcending
the reality of night and nothingness. We forget that each one
of us in his personal life repeats that miracle...We are in a
creative universe. Let us then create.

Loren Eiseley

If someone should ask me, "What does the soul *do*?"
I would say, It loves. And it creates.

Sue Monk Kidd

Let us hope it will always be like this, each of us
going on in our inexplicable ways building the universe.

Mary Oliver

The diaphany of the divine
at the heart of the universe on fire.

Teilhard de Chardin

(at the magical hour when is becomes if)

E. E. Cummings

CONTENTS

AUTHOR'S FOREWORD

R etirement for one privileged and still healthy offers wondrous opportunities. Like for instance to rise early and sit either before a woodstove fire in the cold months or, when it's warmer, in a circle of stones in the nearby woods to await the sun's rising. And do what? Just wait for things to pop up. Call me a ponderer with pad and pen. A glance through Contents will reveal the variety of things that popped up for this octogenarian ponderer who sees himself as reaching out to other spirit-journeying ponderers, likely also to be in the second half of their journey.

Be Creative and Live Forever is actually the fourth in a series of ruminations, each covering roughly a year, begun at a hard time for the world with the outbreak of the pandemic and a hard time for my family with leukemia invading the body of my grandson. Where the most recent book, *Glimmerings and Stammerings*, left off in May of 2023, the present volume picks up.

Runner-ups for possible titles of this volume: Deep Down We are Fire, God Has Never been Here Before, Don't Take it to the Grave, Take a Deep Dive into Empathy, The Throbbing Universe a Machine?, Before You Knock Progressives, Plug into the Current, and Had Jesus Gotten to be an Old Guy. Just to whet your appetite.

As for the subtitle, I think of twilight as amorous. Do not light and dark, at those two liminal times in each 24-hour cycle, melt magically into each other in their fleeting embrace? Perfect time, the twilight, for ruminating on things that pop up from memory and imagination.

My take on novels (what worlds they open up!) is that, being horizontal, they invite settling in for the long haul, savoring a story's suspenseful unfolding—the longer the better if it's a good one! With poems it is different given that their stories (yes, each poem has one) are vertical, inviting the reader to slow down and go deep. Consider the ruminations that follow as invitations to slow down and go deep.

Spirit journeyers, come. Relish to know you have company.

INTRODUCTION

A s each poem in this volume stands alone, it is not necessary to proceed in the chronological order that it was written. You may wish simply to glance through the Contents section, pick out a few titles that intrigue, and then check these poems out to see if there is resonance. If not you will realize this is not your cup of poetry. But if there *is* a resonance, even more if you find something that strikes fire, hopefully you will honor that flame and explore further.

But you may choose instead to start at the beginning, in May of 2023, carrying through to May of 2024. My ruminations on multiple things, external as well as internal, likely will prompt ruminations of your own during this difficult time for our nation and the world.

At poetry readings I have found it helpful when the poet would make a few comments before each poem to set the stage for what's coming, placing it in a context that might hopefully whet interest. I've followed suit with the poems in this volume introducing each with a comment that, along with the title, might serve as a lure. Poetry and fishing have things in common. No possible bite without a lure.

One might think I'm out there alone.

Come on Now

Out in the woods
doesn't mean out alone.
I mean, come on now—
think birds, think trees,
think forest awash with presence! 5/14/23

How pleased I am I didn't give up on it too soon.

Tempted to Put Demon Copperhead Down

Early into Demon Copperhead
I'm tempted to put it down—
too much pain pure and simple.
Barbara Kingsolver gets that part right.
But knowing what else she gets right
in her other heart-soaring books
encourages me to keep on.
Redemption of the heart I trust is coming. 5/14/23

Gray clouds this morning
haven't quieted the choir—
it must be the light! 5/15/23

Most folks are not Friends (what Quakers call themselves) but perhaps are curious.

Quaker Haiku

Sitting in silence
is how some Quakers worship.
Ever wonder why? 5/16/23

Escaping the noise
and a thousand distractions—
best way to listen. 5/16/23

Simple as it sounds
it is harder than you think.
Who knows what you'll hear? 5/16/23

Expectant waiting
is how Friends like to put it—
alert for Spirit. 5/16/23

Things long avoided
tend to rise to the surface.
Who says there aren't ghosts? 5/16/23

The trickiest part—
discerning whether to rise
to give a message. 5/16/23

Dropping a pebble
sends ripples across the pond,
no telling how far. 5/16/23

Pondering the vastness of Wisdom.

Calling at Every Bend in Your River

Wisdom, what does it mean to you,
and how did you come by
whatever measure you might possess?
And who at every bend
of your life's winding river
has stood waving on the shore
embodying it for you?
If the word itself lacks allure,
think Sapientia or Sophia
calling at every bend.
What is she calling?
How will you answer? 5/18/23

Like it or not traumas will come.

The Best We Can Do

Traumas endured and learned from
is the best we can do,
trusting with the support
of the community of our friends
there's nothing we can't get through. 5/24/23

No one is exempt when it comes to trauma.

Scar Tissue

Remembering there is scar tissue
over every beating heart
should help with compassion.
It's a rough journey. 5/24/23

A line from a poem that has taken root.

Nothing Beautiful Ever Hurries

"Nothing beautiful ever hurries."
I like imagining E. E. Cummings
hushed in a temple of trees. 5/25/23

Another way of saying that love's a very big deal.

Stand-in for God

Think of yourself
as a stand-in for God
whenever you cherish.
Is there anyone in the world
who doesn't yearn to be cherished? 5/25/23

No wonder we fear it until we look closer.

Imagine Death Your Dearest Friend

Decry death all you want,
but can you imagine the Dance without it?
Rather than the ultimate foe lurking,
imagine it your dearest friend
shaking you by the shoulders till you wake
and create something beautiful while you can. 5/25/23

A way to start the day.

Marching Orders for Today

Pay close attention,
amazing things are afoot.
Spread the Smile.
You're it. 5/26/23

Is the universe an It or a Thou? Is there a more important question?

Caught Up in a Thou

What if it's not only all interconnected
but not an it?
How *could* it be if we're included?
To be caught up in a Thou—
wow! 5/26/23

Be a sunflower.
Let others feel your turning
toward their bright presence. 5/26/23

Such early morning company, with or without names.

Exemplary Distinction

The Vireos are having at it,
Red-eyed and Yellow-throated,
as they serenade the morning.
Thanks to my bird app
with names now they're not just birds
but persons each with distinct voice!
So too trees surrounding
whispering (thanks to wind)
their own exemplary distinction. 5/27/23

Be ready to pay a price if you leave behind doctrine.

A Necessary Price to Pay

Prepare as your faith extends
beyond indoctrinated channels
to be an enigma if not a threat
to those comfortable in the channels—
a necessary price to pay
in exchange for the welcoming
from those who comprehend,
cheering your courage and vision. 5/27/23

I have a framed photo of a feather under which are the floating words, "I have all the time I need," a saving reminder when "there just isn't enough time!"

All the Time I Need

I have all
the time
I need.
Many times these feathery words
have slowed me down.
One step at a time.
All will be well. 5/28/23

I like imagining Buddha and Jesus dancing with Shiva.

Fear not Black Holes

Quantum field,
fertile vacuum,
particles popping up from nowhere
as fast disappearing,
Shiva creating,
Shiva destroying.
Such firing at the heart of stone and me.
The message?
Fear not black holes
with light guaranteed to return. 5/28/23

The human heart, how is it not one heart removed from the heart of the universe? Does it not stand to reason?

Off Goes My Mind Spinning

How layered with grieving, our hearts,
how layered with love.
Can anything in all the universe
that we yet are aware of
be more complex than the human heart?
Off goes my mind spinning
in the direction of the *universe's* heart—
if all is of a piece,
how not of a Person
not done yet with birthing! 5/29/23

May we each have such companions

When Poets Take Hold

"The most comforting speech in the world"—
Thomas Merton's words come back soothing
as I listen to the morning rain.
Then Hopkins adds his plaintive cry,
"Mine, O thou lord of life, send my roots rain."
Poets when they take hold
become companions for life. 5/29/23

Following intoxication to the far reaches.

Intoxicating to Her Core

Jesus was God-intoxicated,
Paul was Christ intoxicated,
Mohammed was Allah-intoxicated,
dervishes were so intoxicated
they had to whirl with it.
Assume not others are less intoxicated
for choosing not to nail a name to Great Mystery.
"Inebriate of air am I
and debauchee of dew"—
thank you, Emily Dickinson,
poets are intoxicated too,
as were Taoists content
to be drunk on the moon.
What other conclusion
than that the Matrix of us all
to which we affix the word universe
is intoxicating to her core! 5/31/23

I call it my predictable inner squabble, more like a subterranean tango in a lifelong dance.

Back and Forth as if on Script

Mouse: "Safer to keep it to myself—
what will they think?"
Moose: "But what opportunity
to give them something *new* to think!" 6/10/23

I'll smile if this paints for you a comforting scene.

Buckley Wins Paws Down

It's quite a friendly arrangement
before the woodstove fire—
my writing pad undulating
atop Buckley's soft breathing.
God herself might be smiling
to wonder who's the more contented.
I'd have to say from his soft breathing
and my unsteady writing,
Buckley wins paws down. 5/30/23

Admiration woven with regret.

Wishing I Gave a Little More

I hear Guatemala sing
from a colorful wall hanging in my Cave
but I also feel a sting
from the memory of the small brown woman
imploring with eyes as much as words
that for three months of her life
I might give for it a little more.
Looking back forty-eight years
at this creation of woven beauty
costing three months of a peasant's life,
I'm wishing I gave a little more. 6/11/23

Mysticism in a nutshell.

Ici le Bon Dieu

Eighteen years ago today at Lisieux
I sat in the basilica of St. Therese
pondering her perfect words:
"Ici le bon Dieu."
I daresay no mystic on Earth
whether religious or not
would fail to fathom. 6/11/23

Children catch the human essence when constantly asking questions.

Questions Mark Us Human

The better questions
have no easy answers,
the best no answer at all.
Why then ask them?
How could we not?
They mark us human. 6/12/23

Bringing the solstice up close and personal.

Standing Still like the Sun

Each time we settle into silence—
standing still like the sun to discern
if it's time to change direction—
are we not reenacting the solstice? 6/14/23

We honor our other grandmothers, don't we?

Without Her Where Would We Be?

You blandly call it a supernova,
I ecstatically call it the explosive giveaway
of our sacrificial Grandmother Star.
Now you tell me,
without her where would we be? 6/13/23

Know thyself sounds tame until you take a day or a year to think about it.

Calling for High Courage

Have we not each
a dark underside
hidden as much
from ourselves as the world?
Know thyself, intones the oracle
calling for high courage. 6/14/23

Is there not a story behind every sound?

Forgiving the Jet

Imagining the joy
of someone heading home
I forgive the jet
for drowning out the birds. 6/25/23

Smooth talkers will never reach the heart.

Hearing a Crack in the Voice

Heads jabber on the surface,
hearts stammer at the threshold
of the realm beyond words' reach.
Don't you love hearing a crack in the voice,
a stammer that is so eloquent
you never forget it? 6/26/23

Think how it would elevate your self-esteem to the point of astonish-
ment to recognize you have an interior castle.

Inner Sanctum

An inner sanctum.
We each have one,
what Saint Theresa called an interior castle—
with chambers spiraling inward,
the innermost for ecstatic union.
Something to ponder
when wondering what your life is about,
or could be. 6/27/23

Remember the power of a written-by-hand letter, or words slowly
spoken with eyes fixed on your own.

Don't Take It to the Grave

Don't we each yearn
to know we are cherished?
Don't take to the grave your cherishing
not yet expressed to another. 6/27/23

Wouldn't it add to the drama if God, too, knew not the future?

God Has Never Been Here Before

You who love a good page-turner
imagine God does too
bent over each next page
of your unfinished story. 6/29/23

Be wary of crusades that begin by banning books.

Fascism's Beachhead

There's mobilization across the land
to rid libraries of books deemed offensive.
Eternal seems the need
to blot out things (or people) that most frighten.
See censorship as fascism's way
of establishing a beachhead. 6/29/23

A coaxing.

The Feel of Velvet

One could do worse
than read a Mary Oliver poem every day.
It has to do with the feel of velvet. 6/29/23

All four gospels highlight an event that launched the Passion narrative, but how reconcile it with the Sermon?

Trying to Figure out Jesus

How to reconcile his sermon on the Mount
with causing that uproar outside the Temple
guaranteed to have consequences—
a question for anyone
trying to figure out Jesus. 6/29/23

Whether given or received, trust is a very big thing.

Trusting and Trusted

When I lean down to my dog
he immediately turns over
to receive a love's rubbing
over just the right place on his chest.
O for him to be so trusting,
me so trusted. 6/29/23

To think each can sing
a lyrical song to God
she hasn't yet heard! 6/29/23

If you're not yet alarmed at the crisis, pray God what will it take?

Do We Need to Gag before We Listen?

Air quality is poor again today,
trying to tell us something.
Do we need to gag before we listen? 6/29/23

To consider the universe nothing but a sprawling "it," might that not be the greatest delusion, also the loneliest?

Organic from the Get-Go

How is the universe object
if we are subject?
Come on now,
can the bush that blossoms
all along have been barren?
Beam to see yourself your favorite flower
emerging from Great Mystery
organic from the get-go! 6/30/23

And you thought you were but a blip on the screen.

Both Ancient and Brand New

13.8 billion years are deep hidden
in the face you see in the mirror—
incomprehensibly ancient
yet spanking brand new! 6/30/23

A grandfather once again!

Dancing with an Angel

I danced with an angel, I swear it.
Eight pounds with shining eyes bright
she flowed with the soft sway
of a dance in the kitchen
in the arms of her Pop Pop
softly singing to his angel.
Never will I forget
a magical day in Ft. Worth
when this grandfather once again
danced with an angel! 7/3/23

Tell about someone
who has expanded your life.
Good way to spread light. 7/7/23

Reflecting on two friends meeting the ultimate challenge.

Relishing Their Time Remaining

I've two close friends
who are living with incurable cancer.
Fully cognizant how precious it is,
they relish their time remaining.
A beautiful word is relish—
filled with deep savoring,
endless thanksgiving. 7/8/23

It takes layers of indoctrination not to see it.

The Single Temple

Disparaging and dispiriting
is the word "supernatural,"
natural then relegated
to lowly handmaiden to the Queen.
But how can the Queen herself not be natural?
Mystical body? Think universe
in which each star, tree and human
carries the same current!
See nature, God included,
as the single temple!
Bring offerings. 7/8/23

Thinking long enough about it, to whom are we not kin?

Flashing Love with Our Lantern

If "chosen" inflates
we've missed the message.
Lightning bugs too
flashing love with their lanterns
by the universe have been chosen.
Are we chance flukes in a maelstrom
or along with lightning bugs chosen
to flash love with our lanterns? 7/8/23

Theologians, see beyond your Book!

The Current Flows Forward

How sad to think revelation
can be found only in a Book
which but serves to freeze it.
The Current flows forward! 7/8/23

Early July in these parts means berrypicking time!

Succulent Lyrical Day

Listening to the Beatles
while picking red raspberries—
can you think of a better way
to spend a succulent lyrical day? 7/8/23

Think of the conditioning that has made this not obvious?

The Stupendous Realization

Assuming the universe
is vast, cold, and "out there"
misses the pulsing warmth
of one of its faces in the mirror.
What if the universe
is you in the process
of waking to the stupendous realization? 7/8/23

Let's just say, without time it's inconceivable.

Static Heaven? Heaven Forbid!

A reincarnationalist friend gently asks—
upon hearing my expectation
that on the other side of the Rainbow Bridge
will be some kind of grand reunion—
"After the party, what then?"
The question it forces me to ponder
is can time really end if we're to keep growing
and if we're no longer growing
who would want that?
Static heaven? Heaven forbid! 7/8/23

You will never know
how far the ripple reaches
from your pebble dropped. 7/10/23

*I was fascinated to learn The Human Phenomenon by Teilhard was
one of the books on Jung's bedside before he bid the world adieu.*

Cosmogonic Love

"This Tremendous Lover"—
line from "The Hound of Heaven"
and title of a book about Jesus
I read long ago in the seminary.
Over the years for me Jesus has morphed
into the Mysterium Tremendum of the cosmos
building love across billions of years.
Did Jung mean something like that
when writing in his memoir
about "cosmogonic love"? 7/10/23

The Mother of the Muses not by chance was named Memory.

Lay Flowers before the Shrine

I won't exhort you to keep a journal
knowing that's not everyone's way
yet I plead to each one reading
somehow to keep laying flowers
before the shrine called Remember. 7/10/23

In case you slip back into feeling you don't count.

Luminous Realization

Your every gesture of love
extends the great project of the universe.
Glow with the power and the glory
of luminous realization! 7/10/23

The difference now knowing their names!

My Birdbath Runneth Over

How my affection for birds grows
now having names for them each!
Before—"What a lovely birdsong,"
now—"Red-eyed Vireo how persistent,
Indigo Bunting how sweet,
Tufted Titmouse, such music for a little guy,
Crow how raucous,
Mourning Dove how poignant,
Pileated Woodpecker how riotous you make the morning,
Mockingbird you're back!"
My birdbath had been full
but now thanks to Merlin
it runneth over. 7/10/23

Think lamp cord, think spiritual practice.

Stay Plugged In

How not receive the charge
once plugged into the current?
The goal of a spiritual practice?
Stay plugged in! 7/11/23

Something to think about next time reticence holds you back.

Sing, Silly!

I am here to give voice
as Thrush in the distance now is doing.
It's not for me to know who'll hear
or what might be made of my song.
What I hear from Thrush is "Sing, silly,
and for Forest's sake don't worry!" 7/11/23

There's no holier word than family, but isn't the real question how far does it reach?

Fear Shrinks the Family

Of course we are programmed for protection,
else why so fearful of strangers?
Search the deeper programming.
In the guise of strangers
spy sisters and brothers!
Fear shrinks the family. 7/11/23

You can get away but still pay a price.

Where a Whiff can Send You

A whiff of skunk
tells me of an encounter in the night—
I find myself hoping the other got away.
But even if so
that other is not only still hungry
but stinketh.
Not an easy way to start the new day. 7/12/23

The simpler the question, the harder the response.

Know Thyself

"Just who do you think you are?"
"Whose are you?"
Which of these questions
do you think prompts a truer response
to the oracle's riddle? 7/12/23

Easy to put this one off. Problem is when the time comes, fog may have set in.

If but a Moment Left to Live

What would you say
if you had but a moment left to live
and to whom would you say it? 7/12/23

Instead of discarding dogmas, give them wings.

Be it Done unto Me

If grace is amazing
for saving a wretch like me,
so is it sanctifying
for being the live current of creation.
Protestants and Catholics alike
live, move, and have their being
in a universe pulsing with grace.
May we feel Mary's presence
at our next annunciation. 7/13/23

I bet I'm not alone.

When Looking up at the Moon

It's not just a haunting
but an aching that I feel
when I look up at the moon.
Is there beauty more stunning,
mystery more alluring?
I smile to feel the presence of my ancestors
when looking up at the moon. 7/13/23

Carolina Wren
breaks suddenly the silence.
Friend rises to speak. 7/15/23

Remembering the Current surging across eons flashes home prayer's potential potency.

Prayer: Simply Plugging In

Putting plug into socket
makes lamp leap alive.
Think of prayer as simply plugging in
to Current waiting, 7/13/23

The younger you are, the more remote this will feel, but if you're lucky you'll get there.

Looking Down on Gnarled Hands

As I look down on gnarled hands—
skin wrinkled and mottled,
fingers twisted, sometimes twitching—
I'm astounded how wonderfully
these gnarled ones have served me
down my twitching and twisting long journey. 7/14/23

Possibility—
try your best to imagine
a more stirring word. 7/22/23

From birdsong to Annunciation.

Interruptions

Carolina Wren is going at it—
what music from one so small!
Wood Thrush's plaintive cry
rises at the end carrying me with it.
Both insistent and persistent
seems Red-eyed Vireo's sermons—
it's like he's onto something biblical
and determined that I listen.
I begin to complain about all the interruptions
(how's a guy to settle into forest silence?)
but then remember a girl whose peace
was seriously interrupted by an angel.
Now it's leaves dripping
with the gift of last night's rain,
then the drone of a plane high above
whisking, I like to think, someone home.
You'd think a guy could get some quiet
out here alone in the woods,
but then I'm reminded of the surprise gifts
that often accompany interruptions.
Back again to Mary
one day minding her own business. 7/14/23

He who saluted sun as brother sprang to mind when I was crossing the Nile.

Leaping with St. Francis

I asked our guide what did they mean,
those markings chiseled onto that boulder
jutting from a bank on the Nile,
and leapt with St. Francis at his answer.
"BEAUTIFUL IS THE HEART OF RA." 7/18/23

The past isn't past, as Faulkner observed, if one's point of view has never changed, but think if it has!

Lesson from a Kaleidoscope

Never cease revisiting your past
in light of new understanding.
Doesn't a kaleidoscope teach
a twist of perspective alters everything? 7/18/23

I suspect those decrying "wokeness" conveniently are forgetting their roots.

Isn't it All About Awakening?

I can't imagine the Baptist
or for that matter Jesus or the Buddha
being alarmed by the word "woke,"
now really, can you?
Isn't it, cost what it may,
all about awakening? 7/18/23

Hardly the Grim Reaper.

Death on My Left Shoulder

Death on my left shoulder—
enemy of all I hold dear
or friend perched there to remind me
to give my gift while I can? 7/21/23

My guess as to which instrument Crow would choose.

A Kettledrum in the Orchestra

I'm wondering if the rest of the birds
get their feathers ruffled by raucous Crow
or instead share my enthrallment
at the commanding presence
of a kettledrum in the orchestra. 7/23/23

What lungs for a little guy.

Ringing on the Wings of the Morning

Small does not mean timid.
Have you ever thrilled to listen
to Carolina Wren's gusto
ringing on the wings of the morning? 7/27/23

Imagination loves to play.

Ruminating on a Woodpecker

I bet Red-bellied Woodpecker
is announcing to the forest this morning
the satisfying fun he's been having
rat-a-tat-tatting the gutter
directly above my bedroom window.
Doubtless all are laughing at his mischief
except for the bedroom's occupant
remembering his vain efforts to sleep
and for the mites in the wood beneath the gutter
who wish they could munch in peace
without dreading being eaten. 7/23/23

I'd say it's past time to sound the alarm.

Do We Really Think They're Bluffing?

"We won't stand for it!" claim eighteen million
armed and dangerous
should his election be stolen again,
should THEIR election be stolen again.
Do we really think they're bluffing,
that the head of the pack isn't huffing and puffing
ready if once again he doesn't win
to blow the house down? 7/26/23

*Thinking back with a shudder to talk radio and Contract with
America.*

When Nastiness became Endemic

Nastiness became endemic
with the likes of Limbaugh and Gingrich
setting the grim stage
for fuller manifestations to follow. 7/27/23

Just think what "kingdom to come" likely triggered.

Herod and Rome weren't Buying It

Thinking of puppet King Herod
of a people under the boot of King Rome,
is there any wonder the threat to both kings
posed by an itinerant preacher
boldly announcing a new kingdom?
"But his kingdom was not of this world."
Herod and Rome weren't buying it
particularly after a triumphal entry
followed by a Temple disturbance. 7/27/23

What's your vow, seeker,
to renew upon rising,
your pure intention? 7/29/23

Relationship is one of those words become dull, until Jung returns the sheen.

When Two Truly Interact

Thinking alchemically,
Jung stressed when two truly interact
each becomes something new—
hardly surprising in a universe
enamored of incessant creation! 7/27/23

As Einstein reluctantly noted, in the mysterious quantum field one simply can't deny "spooky action at a distance."

Praying for someone
catapults courage and peace
through grace-channeled space. 7/31/23

Who says light and dark don't quiver in anticipation of each twilight's next trysting?

Till Twilight's Next Trysting

Onset of evening's dark,
then morning's first light—
imagine lovers intermingling
then softly taking leave
till twilight's next trysting. 8/3/23

Aiming for perspective.

A Remarkable Day

Did you lift a burden today,
make someone smile for feeling noticed, feeling
    important?
Did you do something well today
beyond slipshod and haphazard,
attentive to details where life is?
Did you pause at intervals today
to breathe in beauty,
breathe out thanksgiving?
If so, fellow pilgrim, I'd say
you had a remarkable day. 8/1/23

Who says old farts can't give birth?

Is There a Baby in There?

While I wouldn't say my pouch is bulging
it must have been hinting of a secret
for a four-year-old visitor to pat it
wondering if there was a baby in there.
I laughed to assure her there wasn't
but then beamed to remember
that with poems I *am* pregnant,
it's just that I hadn't realized
just where they might be hiding
dreaming of emergence. 8/14/23

Of course we must each have a call.

The Marvel of Recognition

No longer do I need Merlin
to tell me the voice I just heard
belongs to Eastern Wood Pewee.
I recognize it!
Neither, I choose to believe,
does the Spirit of the universe
called by a thousand names
need an app to recognize
the voice belonging to us each. 8/15/23

Pondering here the connection between prayer and love.

Trysting with Great Mystery

If the universe is friendly,
meaning inclining in the direction of love,
would then not prayer be a tryst
with none other than Great Mystery? 8/15/23

Would not this, but a few years ago, have been inconceivable?

Imagine Something Precious Lost

G. K. Chesterton was fond of saying
we don't fully appreciate something
until we imagine it lost.
Have we ever in our lifetime
appreciated democracy more? 8/16/23

Track down this Joe Cocker song and be stunned to re-imagine the singer.

Another Angle on Prayer

"You are so beautiful to me"
is the way Joe Cocker
began his long ago lovesong.
Imagine hearing those words
sung by the heart of the universe
believe it or not to you!
Would not prayer then
simply be singing them back? 8/16/23

Who says they're gone?

Vault of Heart, Tower of Memory

Thanks to vault of heart and tower of memory,
those beyond tactile reach
hardly are distant.
Imagine one cherished and presumed gone
leaning close,
speaking heart to heart,
only asking that you listen. 8/16/23

Venom for venom—
how not a scenario
for a true snakepit? 8/17/23

Thinking hard about two events.

Like any Holy Word

Thinking of the Capitol
calls to mind true patriots
whose courage at the cost of their lives
diverted a missile intended to level it,
and a group *calling* themselves patriots
ransacking it with glee.
Like any holy word
patriotism can be desecrated. 8/18/23

Not one of us is exempt from the creativity (ever since Big Bang blast off) that still courses through the stupendous still-birthing.

Who Knows What We Might Create?

Imagine Vincent before a blank canvas,
Michelangelo before a marble block,
or Yeats heading out to the hazel wood
with a fire in his head.
Who knows what each of us,
aligned with the universe (a.k.a. God)
might create by our courage or kindness
this golden new day? 8/19/23

Bright apparition—
red gladiolus chalice
stunning in the sun. 8/20/23

A wonderful Native prayer invokes "all our relations," extending far beyond the two-leggeds.

The Dogs in Your Life

Right away you smile to remember them,
how could you not?
Absolutely they were family!
Lift your heart to imagine
a reunion with each. 8/19/23

Would they really have come empty-handed??

That Day on the Hillside

Could the miracle that day on the hillside
have been that literally thousands
were so moved by his love-sermon
that they dug deep in their knapsacks
making sure no one went home hungry? 8/20/23

Can we allow there might be an angle we've been missing?

When a Discordant Note Jars

When a discordant note jars
our echo chamber comfort,
do we stop to consider
if there's an angle we've been missing
or promptly revert to dismissing
with barely concealed hissing? 8/22/23

Beyond even Bold.

Audacious
Feel your heart reigniting
simply to gaze on the word "audacious."
For you what would that mean? 8/23/23

*The quote is from the Foreword to The Human Phenomenon by
Teilhard de Chardin.*

Behind the Workings of the Universe

"To see or to perish is the very condition
laid upon everything that makes up the universe."
What did Teilhard himself see
behind the workings of the universe?
Amorization—
fire ignited in the beginning
traveling eons toward love! 8/26/23

Lest we get smug.

Parable to Bring Us to Our Knees

How not fall on our knees begging mercy
if we take to heart his parable
about the least of these? 8/25/23

What are cooks but alchemists in the kitchen?

Every Meal Reenacts the Cosmos

Can't get my head around it—
particles popping up out of nowhere then vanishing.
"Quantum soup" is actually an apt metaphor—
thick savory gumbo
conjured by a chef out of sight
with seasonings and spices from us each!
No wonder the pleasure of cooking—
every meal reenacts the cosmos! 8/26/23

Helpless pawns we are not.

Possibility and Opportunity

Words have power.
Two coming to my rescue this morning
as niggling worries assail
are possibility and opportunity—
the first flings open every window,
the second, however dire the circumstance,
invites imagination. 8/29/23

Ah, back to the enigma of meaning.

When Meanings Emerge

Looking back to gain perspective
changes not facts but meanings.
Could you have reached where you are
without each turn and twist,
detour and blind alley,
crushing loss and surprise gain?
Do not meanings emerge
only when we look back? 8/30/23

If it looks like I'm out there all alone…

Companionable in the Woods

It's companionable out here in the woods—
beyond birds, squirrels and trees
it's all who have emboldened
my life with their love.
How can they not be here too? 8/31/23

*"The moral arc of the universe bends toward justice" doesn't come
without a moral imperative.*

Has Justice Ever Not Needed Help?

What weight are you lending
to the bending of the arc?
Has justice ever not needed help? 9/6/23

Make room for whimsy.

Love Call, not Sermon

When I mentioned that Red-eyed Vireo
dubbed by me Rev for his incessant sermons
was no longer to be heard,
my wife smiled and said what it likely means
is that his sermons were really love calls
and someone in the pews finally answered.
It's happy imagining him busy now
building a nest for little ones on the way
trusting it will be time again next summer
to climb back into the pulpit.
Better explanation is he took off for the winter,
but whimsy prefers this one. 9/8/23

Challenge the status quo? Be willing to pay the price.

Moving the Needle toward Justice

Have not progressives (a.k.a. prophets)
always gotten a harsh rap
for their infuriating righteousness,
their discontentment with the way things are?
Can you point to a single advancement
in the direction of greater justice
for underdog person or planet
where progressives didn't pave the way
contemned for their doggedness?
Maybe someday we'll honor abolitionists
for their vision and their valor. 9/11/23

If you feel the pride you've gotten the message.

Groping for Adequate Words

Challenges faced and overcome,
focused mind,
skilled hands,
tenderness of heart,
and now dreams for the daughter
cradled in his arms.
Just a father groping for adequate words
to salute his son. 9/15/23

For when I'm feeling small and frightened.

Pep Talk

No feather in the wind,
how about letting go the fears?
Behind you are nothing less
than fourteen billion cosmic years! 9/17/23

Stops me every time—
train whistle in the distance
stirring something deep. 9/20/23

The next two relate to my Earth emergence.

No Day More Revelatory

On this day long ago
my lungs first took in air,
my eyes blinded by light
first beheld eyes adoring,
my body first felt arms embracing,
my lips first tasted milk's sweetness.
Now you tell me,
can any day be more revelatory
than the day of such firsts? 9/21/23

Funny the things that stay with you across a lifetime.

Ha, You Thought I Just Turned 82

Dad were he still here
would have reminded me this morning
that I've begun my 83rd.
As a kid I'd be flummoxed—
"What do you mean I've begun my 8th?
I just turned 7!"
He'd smile now as he did then
having announced not end but beginning.
Ha, you thought I just turned 82—
actually I've begun 83! 9/21/23

Call this an attempt to retrieve primal wonder.

Pinch Me, was I Dreaming?

You're not going to believe this.
There I was surrounded by darkness
when slowly trees all around me
against faintest gray background
began to take shape!
And the light kept getting stronger
till on East's horizon what blazed forth
was a disc of fire!
Pinch me, was I dreaming? 9/28/23

A gesture can make all the difference.

When Trying to Reach One Fortressed

As your heart bends in compassion
toward one imprisoned in darkness,
pray for the right words
(let heart take the lead)
that might sneak a streak of light
through a chink in the fortress.
Fists stand not a chance
but a gesture just might with God's grace
penetrate with a streak. 9/28/23

Regardless your faith,
will the future be sweetened
by your compassion? 9/28/23

"Way will open" is a time-honored Quaker expression of radical trust in the universe, not unlike what I had been discovering in my journey to the East following my departure from organized religion.

Way will Open

Thirty-seven years ago today
sitting in the silence of my first Meeting for Worship
in a small chapel on the Hollins College campus
in mountain-encircled Roanoke Virginia,
a woman diminutive but dynamic
softly thundered words riveting:
WAY WILL OPEN.
Journeying East since departing from Catholicism,
I raced home to write in my journal,
"That's Taoism!" 9/22/23

Cosmic Alchemist
working from the inside out—
think evolution. 9/30/23

Long friendship—just savor the words.

Of All Life's Gifts

On the docket for today—
a gathering of old guys
sounding barbaric yawps with Whitman
across the rooftops of the world.
Of all life's gifts is there a sweeter
than long friendship? 9/29/23

There are, pure and simple, not enough poems about the moon.

Spellbound before Her Full Beauty

Were the moon full each night
we'd fast take her for granted,
ho-hum that bright orb in the night.
Ah, but since she's but a fraction of herself every night
    in the month but one
(and at a dark time in the month flat gone),
is it any wonder we find ourselves
on that single night in the whole month
in the company of our ancestors
spellbound before her full beauty? 9/29/23

Staying with beauty.

Be on the Lookout Today

Be on the lookout today
for beauty stopping you in your tracks,
taking away your breath
if only for a second.
A few such seconds
could make your day! 9/29/23

I close my eyes and I'm back there!

Sapphire Apparition

Nine years it's been
since looking down on the stunning blue
of a water-filled crater
blasted into being long ago
by a colossal volcanic eruption.
Please if you make it to southern Oregon
circle upward till you're gasping
to look down on the sapphire apparition
called Crater Lake! 9/30/23

A new month begins
for each of us this morning.
How lucky is that? 10/1/23

How is it not a red-letter day to receive a new name?

Building an O Bridge

Leave it to my granddaughter of five
to create for me a new name
by simply building an o bridge
between each of my Pops.
Thanks to Mari I'm now Pop-o-Pop! 9/30/23

The phrase was a favorite of Howard Thurman.

What We Listen For

The sound of the genuine—
isn't that what we listen for
when we listen to another? 10/1/23

Here's betting you remember vividly when someone spoke from the heart.

Speaking from the Heart

A man just gave such witness
to a woman impacting his life
that when mentioning at the end
she had just succumbed to a disease
we were all seized with grieving.
What power when one speaks from the heart! 10/1/23

Logic makes a case
the cosmos is a brute place,
but what about love? 10/2/23

Regarding your identity...

Through You to Who Knows Where

Think not immanence here
and transcendence there—
dualism misses the glory!
Think *immanence transcending*
ever since the Big Bang
reaching up through creation to very you
and through you to who knows where! 10/3/23

Naming makes a difference.

Gaia's Temple

Try to think of something not natural.
You can't.
Take ten seconds each hour
to salute wherever your eyes land upon,
greet wherever your feet meet
our Mother whom our ancestors named Gaia.
Does not every single one of us
live, move, and have our being
in Gaia's temple? 10/3/23

All in one day.

Humming Ode to Joy All Day

From Lipizzaner ecstasy
to abodes of Beethoven and Freud—
no mystery why it stays with me,
that day in Vienna long ago,
when I couldn't stop humming Ode to Joy. 10/4/23

You never know where you'll end up.

As Protestant as You can Get

When growing up Catholic
Protestants were always the bad guys
jealous of our longer history,
trying to bring us down.
Imagine my astonishment to realize
after gravitating years later to the Quakers
that where I had ended up
was as Protestant as you can get!
May my parents be seeing a broader picture
and not turning in their graves. 10/4/23

Fur person (May Sarton's affectionate term) does far more justice than pet.

Buckley's Arrival Day

Two years ago to the day
a Pomeranian pooch arrived
to become no mere pet
but true member of the family.
Many smile to comprehend. 10/4/23

An octogenarian's prayer at twilight time.

Twilight Prayer

My prayer as I drift through twilight
(is any time more stirring?)
is to be fortified beyond fright
as I advance toward the night. 10/4/23

Console yourself to know that the little it may seem that you do is exactly that much more than would have been done without you.

Beats Saying to Hell with It

I can't fix the world
but won't being kind today to those I meet
nudge it in the right direction?
Beats saying to hell with it. 10/5/23

Track down Joe Cocker's love song, and see where it can lead.

You are so Beautiful to Me

"You are so beautiful to me"—
Joe Cocker nailed it
with his lyrical love song,
but dare to take it higher.
Wouldn't God, too, love to hear it?
Then imagine if you can
hearing from the heart of the universe
this exact same lyrical love song
sung to *you*. 10/5/23

The effort required to get to the Matterhorn is massively rewarded.

Ecstasy Awaits at Zermatt

Imagine riding a cog railway up and up
finally to arrive in a small Alpine village
disallowing motorized vehicles
to enhance the quietude and the magnitude
of standing spellbound before the apparition
of the Horn of Matter!
Travelers to southern Switzerland,
ecstasy awaits at Zermatt. 10/11/23

It's a solemn moment, approaching the great crossing. Here are my wishes for my friend.

Dipped Again in God and New Created

A friend across decades informed me
he has just entered hospice,
all attempts to halt the advance having failed.
I wish him calm trust.
I wish him cherished memories
of all who have blessed his journey,
been blessed *by* his journey,
who stand silent on the shore
with full hearts as his ship
readies to embark for the last horizon.
Carrying with him all his loves,
may in the words of D. H. Lawrence
he quietly trust he will soon
"be dipped again in God and new created." 10/11/23

Refrain of mystics across Earth: the kingdom is at hand!

Ici

"Ici le bon Dieu" exclaimed the Little Flower
enamored of the flower of the moment
where she kept finding le bon Dieu. 10/6/23

What I listen for when I listen to another's story.

Listen for Flashpoints

When I'm hearing another's story,
rather than trying to connect all the dots
in order to grasp the full picture
I listen for flashpoints
beaming from eyes, rising in voice.
When the story then is over,
I share what I spied in eyes and voice
and watch the eyes beam again,
the voice rise again
for the joy of being heard! 10/13/23

I'm sure there are many other options, but these at least cover some basics.

Imagining What's behind Each

I'm hungry.
I'm horny.
I'm happy.
It's fun imagining what's behind
each birdsong in the morning. 10/13/23

There's something about
the holiness of twilight
that makes my soul sing. 10/13/23

What you create now
adds to *cosmic* creation—
now think about that! 10/13/23

Can you deny terrifying is the right word?

Terrifying

Terrifying still in Ukraine,
terrifying now in Gaza and Israel
on the brink of terrifying more—
unleashed once again are the dogs of war.
Most terrified are the children,
their parents utterly helpless. 10/14/23

How not shudder?

Can You Conceive a Greater Dilemma?

Either leave everyone behind who can't come,
every cherished possession you can't carry
as you flee for your life with the likelihood
you'll end up homeless if not murdered
or stay put where the risk is near certain
you'll be buried under rubble.
You may conceive of a greater dilemma,
I can't. 10/15/23

A case for the primacy of imagination.

What If?

I submit for your consideration
that the two most hopeful words
regardless the impasse you find yourself at
are *what if.* 10/15/23

Sometimes we have to turn the TV off.

Stop, Empathy!

Heart-rending to think of it
much less see it nightly on TV,
what must it be…?
Stop, empathy!
lest we be swallowed up
buried with them in the rubble.
Find a child to play with,
animal to caress,
tree to listen under,
bird to carry us for the moment
into the peaceful wild blue.
Then come back to consider
if there's any action, however small, we might make
besides praying God have mercy. 10/16/23

CHARLES C. FINN

Yield here to your imagination.

Billions of Years Dreamed

Give the universe a name
(for once make it feminine).
Imagine her pleasure with your emergence
billions of years in her dreaming. 10/15/23

Think your own dreaming
is the universe dreaming—
are you not her child? 10/15/23

My Pomeranian is patient but only to a point.

Cease with the Navel Contemplation!

By standing on my chest
Buckley informs me it's time
to cease with the navel-contemplation.
May we each have a sentient being
to bring us to our senses. 10/16/23

Everywhere we look
the Earth we love is burning.
O Lord, hear her prayer. 10/16/23

Seems not enough dignified, but did he not say it?

Just Hanging out with God

I'm thinking of the phrase "hanging out"
as in friends just enjoying each other's company.
It calls to mind Jesus telling his disciples
he's calling them now friends.
Which gets me wondering
if a good way to view prayer
might be to just hang out with God,
both enjoying each other's company. 10/19/23

Ah, but what of the battles in the night?

Keeping Company with God

On my better nights of tossing and turning
I'm comforted to remember
this is as good a place as any
to keep company with God
herself likely tossing and turning
given all the hardened hearts
and wars and such. 10/20/23

Thinking about Rumi and Jesus, it struck me neither of them needed a pen.

Whirling Fire down the Ages

Rumi calls to mind Jesus.
Neither wrote down a word
preferring to sing as they danced
trusting others would get enough of it down
to whirl fire down the ages. 10/19/23

Thank you, Yeats—such gems in Sailing to Byzantium.

Be not Deceived by Tattered Coats

You wonder why these old guys,
tattered coats on sticks,
keep making time to come together?
It has everything to do with their souls
loving to clap hands and sing
and sing again of their friendship.
No paltry thing. 10/20/23

Whatever you do
don't disdain politicians—
we need the wise ones. 10/21/23

Don't some words open to vastness, like vast itself?

"Vast" Stirs Yearning

What is it about the word vast
that so stirs yearning?
I'm thinking of night sky,
cathedral forest,
feelings at twilight,
a love departed now residing
in a vast inner chamber. 10/21/23

Sometimes you have to turn the set off.

Tonight it was Too Much

Much as we love Ken Burns
we had to turn this one off.
Some things are just too painful.
First it was the mass slaughter of the buffalo
left hideless and tongueless
in heaps rotting in the sun,
then a whole village slaughtered
for having the gall not to like it.
I'll likely see the rest of it later—
how else hope to learn from history?—
but tonight it was too much,
too reminiscent of innocent Israelis at a festival,
innocent Gazans bracing for slaughter. 10/22/23

Turnabout is foul play.

Witchhunt!

"Lock her up, lock her up!"
With glee they meant it.
"Lock him up, lock him up!"
How dare they persecute our leader.
"Witchhunt!" 10/22/23

Find one who has searched the harbor in the night before you.

Lighthouse Spirit Guide

Rejoice that land is near
but the shoals are treacherous—
heed the danger!
Find a lighthouse spirit guide
worthy of the calling. 10/22/23

And you thought you were but a blip on the screen?

Ye Gods that Includes Me

Through the human
the universe is waking up—
ye gods that includes me! 10/24/23

Musing on my granddaughter's 5th birthday.

Layered Now with Hard-won Wisdom

I'll have you know my granddaughter
is five years old this very day—
can we remember the awe when looking up
to see the stars dancing?
Could the whole of life's journey
in some mysterious circuitous way
(factoring in all the disenchantments)
be a preparation for a *deeper* innocence
where layered now with hard-won wisdom
we will in awe again look up
to see the stars are *still* dancing? 10/25/23

An early morning's companionable musing.

I Count among My Friends the Trees

I count among my friends the trees
and the squirrels scrambling in their branches
and scurrying at their feet,
and the birds of course too—
you should hear them waking.
And just this morning a young doe
came nibbling within thirty feet,
checking me out but deeming me harmless
as you would a silent friend.
"Pathetic fallacy!" will shout academics
certain that I'm out here in the woods
sitting all alone. 10/26/23

Do you really think God sees it all in advance? Where's the suspense in that?

Not Even God Knows

A new day stretches before me.
Not even God knows what I'll do with it,
so I like to imagine her cheering me on
sitting on the edge (in my heart)
of her throne. 10/26/23

You might start with The New Cosmic Vision.

Religion, the Tip of the Vanguard

A new meteor across my skies,
John Haught dazzles
following the comet of Teilhard.
It has to do with religion deemed dying
actually being the tip of the vanguard
of the universe still birthing! 10/26/23

If according to Emerson "every word was once a poem," "feeling" is truly an epic.

The Flowering of Feeling

"Pathetic" is one of those words
(from "pathos" meaning capable of feeling)
that sings the deeper you try to fathom it.
The vast venture of the universe—
think of it as the flowering of feeling! 10/26/27

No wonder evolution threatens fundamentalism.

Revelation Done With?

Revelation is over and done with, you say?
How if the universe itself is not done with?
10/27/23

Gazans on my mind.

Is the Blame All Theirs?

People stuck in a ghetto
with no way out
sometimes do horrendous things.
Is the blame all theirs?
Can you not imagine
yourself doing horrendous things
were you stuck in a ghetto
with no way out? 10/27/23

Those claiming the universe is without meaning really mean it.

Now Wait a Second

They mindfully assure us
that the universe is mindless.
They freely insist
that in a purposeless universe
there's room for neither purpose nor freedom.
Go figure. 10/28/23

Anniversaries help us remember.

Gifts of Mind and Spirit

Such gifts he left behind
thirty-six years ago on this day
when bidding us farewell—
among them *The Power of Myth*,
The Hero with a Thousand Faces,
The Inner Reaches of Outer Space,
and *Myths to Live By*.
Such gifts you left us, Joseph Campbell,
of mind and spirit! 10/30/23

Heed ghosts and goblins.
It's their clandestine mission
to scare us to life. 10/31/23

A reconsideration of the place of religion.

Revere Your Religious Heart

Religion at heart means yearning
to bind everything into one sheaf
and now to realize thanks to science
that the sheaf of the universe itself
like a loaf is still rising!
Revere the religious heart within you. 10/28/23

My version of ancestor worship.

Quiet Heart to Hearts

Within a huge poster board circle
are names in bright colors
of significant people in my life
who have crossed the Rainbow Bridge
only to take up permanent residence
in a deep chamber of my heart.
Tomorrow being the Day of the Dead
I'll sit before the comfort of my circle
and have a quiet heart to heart
with each of the names in bright color
whose existence has added richness to my life.
I tingle in anticipation
of quiet heart to hearts
awaiting me tomorrow. 10/31/23

From Mary Oliver's poem "Praying" in her book entitled Thirst.

A Doorway into Thanks

"Just pay attention
then patch a few words together
and don't try to make them elaborate,
this isn't a contest but a doorway into thanks,
and a silence in which another voice may speak."
Just a glimpse into why
I read Mary Oliver daily. 10/31/23

NICU, short for Neonatal Intensive Care Unit, is truly a cause for celebration.

Home after Six Frightful Days

Before there was a NICU
most little ones in dire straits
simply would not have made it
including our granddaughter beyond precious
thankfully able five years ago today
to come home from the NICU
after six frightful days. 10/31/23

Remember when crushed
you let it not defeat you.
When next crushed hang on. 11/1/23

On the occasion of my son's wedding.

Cheering a Great Leap

Folks have come from far and wide
to celebrate two taking the great leap.
Thank you, Adam and Brittney, for bringing us together
reminding us of love, faith and hope
as we cheer your great leap. 11/2/23

A whole different life if I hadn't overheard.

My Ears Perked Up

Feeling fatigued I almost didn't go
to that graduate party long ago
where by chance I overhead a young woman
tell a friend she was lonesome.
My ears, as they say, perked up
and somehow I found my way next to her
for most of the rest of the evening
and as it turned out
for all of the rest of my life.
No matter my hearing has diminished of late,
it was sharp when it was needed. 11/1/23

Blasphemy or good news?

Today Be God

God wraps in a bundle what has been,
then creates something new—
is this not the way of the universe?
In her image and likeness
feel your whole life wrapped in a bundle
ready to create today something new. 11/3/23

A cliché has become reality.

The Election of Our Lifetime

"The election of our lifetime"—
if true in 2020
how not truer in 2024?
Has democracy in the US of A
ever been in more peril?
Come to think of it there was 1860—
fraught with consequence,
to the edge of the precipice and then over.
Not inconceivably we could be there again.
Fervently we pray democracy stiffens,
true patriots rise to the rescue. 11/3/23

Florence calls you for this if nothing else, but there is so much else.

There's Nothing like the First Time

I've been there since
but there's nothing like the first time.
Forty-five years ago today
in awe I stood before the wonder
of a gleaming male body—
that steady gaze at Goliath,
that rock ready in his sling. 11/3/23

Think electricity.

Sharing the Identical Current

Try to get your head around this one.
The universe and you
share the identical current,
are not separate things.
Think connected at the hip,
think image and likeness. 11/3/23

How learn from history if it's buried?

I Honestly Can't Imagine

If I have difficulty watching
Ken Burns' "The American Buffalo"
more than fifteen minutes at a time
for the pain and outrage of it,
what would it be like I wonder
were my skin red?
I honestly can't imagine. 11/4/23

With branches now bare
squirrel acrobatics astound
heretofore hidden. 11/7/23

Do we not cherish moments when we were rapt?

Remembering Maya

Because she was,
we can be better.
Twenty-five years ago today
at Sweetbriar College in Virginia
I sat rapt as I listened
to a phenomenal woman
holding the audience in her hand
as she inspired in equal measure
both our laughter and our tears.
Because she was,
we can be better. 11/4/23

It's a little dismaying how close they will come.

While Honored Still I Worry

A grazing buck draws closer
checking me out but deeming me safe
holding pen and not gun.
While honored still I worry.
It's open season
and not all of my kind are poets. 11/7/23

It's unclear who was more startled.

Rustling Gets My Attention

When I'm out waiting for sun's rising
rustling behind me gets my attention.
Almost without exception
it will be bird, squirrel, turkey or deer,
but a couple times I've been given a start
to see black bear ambling closer
then scrambling back into the woods
when I suddenly stood up.
Heart settling down,
I went back to waiting for the sun. 11/7/23

Amorization is what the universe is about, so said Teilhard. Now there's a vision!

Trust the Current and then Love

Teilhard thought of it as a current
coursing from the get-go toward love
reaching across eons to you and me
called by virtue of our being here
to allow the current to carry us forward.
All we need do
is trust the current and then love! 11/15/23

If you have friends who altered your destiny, wouldn't they love hearing it?

Destiny Night

It's all your fault, Kevin,
for putting your feelings to song.
No less your fault, Ken,
for making words on a page sing.
Without your interfused inspirations
I never would have gone home to write
a letter altering the actual trajectory
of the rest of my life. 11/15/23

Carlos Castaneda was an anthropologist reporting things he learned from a Yaqui sorcerer named Don Juan.

Perhaps the Goal of a Mindful Life

Be ready, Don Juan advised Carlos,
to seize the cubic centimeter of chance
upon which one's destiny may hinge.
These enigmatic words come back
forty-eight years after the evening
when I dared throw my heart into a letter
destined to alter everything thereafter.
Perhaps the goal of a mindful life
is to be ready to seize
the always unexpected
cubic centimeter of chance. 11/15/23

The medium is the message, a wise one once said.

Before Your Fingers Start Pecking

There's a huge difference
between slowly writing a letter
and whipping off an email.
The words may be the same
but they will be read differently.
If it's from the head
an email will serve well,
but if it's from the deep heart,
before your fingers start pecking
you might want to reconsider.
You likely don't save old emails
but I bet you do old letters. 11/16/23

Acolyte singing here.

Will o' the Wisp and Granite

Will o' the wisp and granite—
the mystery and power of words!
Think of those written to you
that have altered your life,
those spoken to you
that either knocked you from your horse
or sent your heart flying.
Take off your shoes before crossing
the threshold to the temple of words. 11/17/23

Don't think Hummingbird, when flitting to the next one, forgets the last flower.

Alchemical Transportation

Teilhard, Lincoln, Frederick Buechner,—
back and forth this past week
I've flitted among all three.
Each alone transporting,
imagine the alchemical transportation
when carried away by the concoction
in my vessel of all three! 11/17/23

It may be fall, but planting is on my mind.

Is There an Autumn Ritual Richer?

The shape, sight and feel
of tulip bulbs planted deep—
is there an autumn ritual richer
than tucking packets of promise into Earth
so she can be dreaming in Technicolor
under winter's drab blanket? 11/19/23

In honor of the date 160 years after.

Seeds planted on graves
(remembering an address)
by sower Lincoln. 11/19/23

Honoring another date.

November 20, 1975

Twoscore and eight years ago
in a bustling Mexican restaurant
where Chicago and Evanston meet,
I plied a young woman with Isabel Rose,
dreams of travel,
and sparkling eyes.
She had prepared at evening's onset
to let me know the time wasn't right
which just goes to show
you should never underestimate the alchemy
of dreams of travel intermixed
with wine and sparkling eyes. 11/20/23

Think big, feel big.

Waifs Adrift? How Sad to Think It

If the universe is out there
vast and impersonal
and we're each here
unquestionably personal,
how not feel we're waifs adrift,
alienated because alien?
But what if we're connected at the hip,
even closer,
to our Mother still birthing?
Waifs adrift? How sad to think it. 11/21/23

Do we not judge a tree by its fruits?

Yardstick to Measure By

It would seem a commendable yardstick
with which to measure one's philosophy or religion
is whether it augments the following:
zest for living,
creativity,
generosity,
gratitude,
kindness,
and not least of all joy.
Whatever your philosophy or religion,
is it not letting you down
if it's not measuring up? 11/26/23

Trying to bring into focus a staggering thing.

The Universe is Waking Up

I'm trying to get my head
around the stupendous fact
that the universe is waking up
on Earth and likely elsewhere too
after billions of years dreaming.
"Self-conscious" is a ho-hum
until lightning strikes—
think what it means! 11/26/23

How is the universe meaningless if today you create something meaningful?

We are not Fated!

"Meaning is not preordained!"
The words fairly shout from a page
in my journal from years ago.
Ten thousand conditionings notwithstanding,
we are not fated!
Bring to the task at hand excellence,
give someone comfort,
spread the gift of your joy.
Feel within you the current
of the very universe on the move
toward greater meaning because of you! 11/27/23

May we lay flowers before Memory's shrine.

Calling Back Fire

There's a bronze statue in Athens—
whether Zeus poised to hurl fire
of Neptune his trident—
that on this day long ago so transfixed me
with the force of its rippling grace
that I'm transfixed still to think of it!
Praised be memory for its power
to call back fire! 11/28/23

Everyone with four-leggeds in the family will understand this one.

May My Friend Find a Measure of Comfort

Husband gone now for years
and daughters on their own,
my friend's sole home companions
have been two cherished dogs
both of whom this past week
she had to put down.
Her sole home companions
just like that gone!
Every heart becomes vulnerable
when taking on love.
May my friend find a measure of comfort
in remembering the home she provided
for two cherished members of her family
over a span of bright years. 11/29/23

Don't rush past this one—never in our country before!

How Tame it used to Sound

How tame it used to sound—
the peaceful transfer of power
where everybody plays by the rules. 12/1/23

What came through this documentary was not politics but humanity.

Transparent of Love's Pain

"Up close and personal"—
a cliché until a documentary
highlights both love and the Constitution
through the eyes and heart of a politician
who returns dignity to the word.
Our democracy if it makes it will be due
to the likes of Jamie Raskin. 11/29/23

When you think of getting older, it doesn't get any better than this.

Something Sacramental

There's something sacramental
about old guys gathering
to follow each other's lead
whether earnest or whimsical
as they cherish a bond forged over years.
Sacramental may seem too holy a word,
but you tell me,
is there anything in the world
holier than long friendship? 12/1/23

Be a large presence
for someone you pass today
hungering kindness. 12/2/23

Churches lead the way for the need for holy days.

And Then We Saw Her Face

Thirty-nine years ago today
we were shown a picture
of an infant girl in Korea
who by the grace of the universe
would soon arrive in our arms.
Penny burst into tears,
my heart soared like an eagle.
And then to learn her Korean name
meant Daughter of the Sun!
Now you see why December 3rd
ever after for us has shouted joy,
stood holy. 12/3/23

Suddenly it was not out of reach.

Pilgrimage across Europe

My trip across Europe long ago
in effect was a pilgrimage to holy ground
where heroes of spirit had breathed.
Fifty-one years ago today
I realized I could make it
all the way to the land called holy
in time for a silent night
where a baby in swaddling clothes
was put after beginning to breathe. 12/5/23

Appalling seems too tepid a word.

Did They not Abandon Ship?

It's appalling to think of election-deniers
still holding office,
breezily planning to run again.
Did they not, however pitiably they spin it,
abandon for personal gain
the Constitutional ship? 12/6/23

Catch the vision!

Carrying Forward the Current

I like to think of Great Mystery
as the Current pulsing through creation
blossoming across billions of years
into feeling,
consciousness,
love!
Be awed to realize
you are here to carry forward the Current
never more than when you love! 12/6/23

Beholding a face
lighting up just to see you—
what validates more? 12/6/23

Let yourself be drawn
by the lure of the Not-Yet.
You are not finished! 12/6/23

How are we not flutes played on by the world wind, drums sending out booming thanks to the world drummer?

Involuntary

Involuntary is a gorgeous word.
Watch your chest rise and fall
without the least effort,
your heart miss nary a beat
without your even needing
to lift a finger. 12/6/23

Consider a pilgrimage.

If You Ever Make it to Rome

For your soul's sake don't miss
if you ever make it to Rome
the Keats Memorial on the Spanish Steps.
"A thing of beauty is a joy forever…
Of nothing do I believe in more
than the holiness of the Heart's affections
and the truth of the Imagination." 12/6/23

What affection scribes
used to have for their candles
deep into the night. 12/6/23

Not sure what triggered this, maybe thinking of Helen Keller.

With Darkness Closing In

Imagine the grief
with darkness closing in
of one going blind
until learning of another's discovery
of a different way to see. 12/6/23

Does not democracy's survival demand it?

When Partisan Opponents Join Forces

I'll tell you what's inspiring—
when partisan opponents
have the wisdom and the courage
to join forces when a crisis
demands it. 12/6/23

If you're ho-hum about the universe, come meet Teilhard de Chardin.

Tag along with Teilhard

From the power of the Once-Was
to the glory of the Not-Yet—
tag along with Teilhard
on the crest of the great wave. 12/6/23

Doesn't this follow if God is love?

God is Full of Feeling

"God is full of feeling"—
words I heard long ago in a homily.
Ridiculous, scoff skeptics,
God's but a human projection.
Ridiculous, scoff dogmatists,
God being perfect must be beyond
the ephemerality of feeling.
But if we know beyond doubt
that beings like ourselves are full of feeling,
why not our Source and Destination
some brazenly call Love? 12/7/23

Ah!

Stunned by the beauty
of a generous spirit,
one word suffices. 12/8/23

Profile of courage
juxtaposed to cowardice—
no doubt which is which. 12/8/23

We have been forewarned.

Ever in Human History?

Has ever in human history
one day of being dictator
satisfied a tyrant? 12/8/23

What greater mystery than whence came the universe?

Let Us Take off Our Shoes Together

I'm as curious as the next guy
about the precise number of years since blast off,
but what rivets my astonishment far more
is who or what lit the fuse?
Can we stop wrangling
over what no one can prove
and take off our shoes together
as we stand agape before the temple entrance
pondering whence the dream
and the spark lighting the fuse? 12/9/23

"Every word," claimed Emerson, "was once a poem." So too
"religion."

Binding into One Sheaf

Religion is one of those words
badly in need of rehabilitation.
Can you think of an impulse more worthy
than to bind into one sheaf
every last loose strand? 12/8/23

What staggering difference between shining and tainted!

Dogma into Metaphor

Hold fast to honoring Mary,
just spread the honor around—
what if each and every one of us
was conceived in blessing and not sin? 12/8/23

Does one massacre
justify an even worse?
No end then to war. 12/9/23

How are we not kin to the Big Bang?

Answering the Thundering Ancient Roar

What if fundamentally nothing
distinguishes you from the Big Bang?
Sink into deep silence
to feel the still pulsing current
from that thundering ancient roar,
then beseech Great Mystery
for the courage to answer
with your *own* thundering roar. 12/14/23

A winter morning's tender ritual.

Alright Already, Buckley, Let's Go

My dog says come on let's go,
my stiff body says I'm not ready.
Perhaps a scritch behind his ears
or a fluff under his chin
will buy me a few more minutes
before this warm fire
and memories from long ago
I'm trying to corral with my pen.
Who am I kidding?
Within seconds I give in.
Alright already, Buckley, let's go! 12/14/23

A special ring is a wondrous thing.

Stone of Africa Reminding Me

The Botswana agate
lodged in a striking silver setting
that called to me in New Orleans
an exact half century ago
has graced my finger since,
stone of Africa reminding me
of the magical mystical place
where the human journey began. 12/14/23

Pondering prayer.

Shape-Shifting Prayer

Some days it's giving thanks,
some days beseeching courage,
some days remembering revelation,
some days begging forgiveness,
some days seeking discernment,
some days crying in anguish
for the suffering of the world.
Then again prayer
some days is just keeping God company,
heart to heart, beyond need for words,
assured deeper than mind can fathom
that all is well. 12/15/23

Call me a pilgrim.

Lured to Crete by Kazantzakis

I'll not deny that I visited Knossos—
how can one not when on Crete?—
but also drawing me like a magnet
was the writing desk in Iraklion
where words were written that fired my soul.
Not on my life would I not visit
on my pilgrimage across Europe long ago
the soil siring Nikos Kazantzakis! 12/15/23

Hyperbole is sometimes called for.

Brace Yourselves, Citizens

There has never in our nation
been an election not touted
as consequential in the extreme,
but really now,
with democracy itself on the ballot,
has anything even remotely rivaled
the election of 2024?
Brace yourselves, citizens,
for possibly the last free US election.
Hyperbole you say?
You must not have been listening. 12/15/23

Is this not the meaning of faith?

More Important than Seeking

More important even than seeking
is the recognition of being sought. 12/16/23

Each next one you love
partially answers your quest
to learn why you're here. 12/18/23

Personality—achievement of billions of years!

Stardust into Persons

Personality's an abstraction
until lightning strikes.
Consider how long it's taken
for the dreaming universe
to turn stardust into persons!
Listen to Jan Christian Smuts
in his Holism and Evolution:
"Personality is the supreme structure
yet reached in Evolution...
the great riddle of the universe...
in it we see matter itself become aglow and luminous
with its own unexpected immanent fire." 12/18/23

A line to ignite your imagination.

Unlocking the Prison Door

"At the magical hour
when is becomes if..."—
so sang E. E. Cummings
unlocking the prison door. 12/19/23

Earth Mother, not on your life a sweet old lady.

Deep down We are Fire

May we never forget we are children
of a Mother whose heart is volcanic—
deep down we are fire! 12/20/23

Staying with fire.

"I Have Come to Spread Fire"

The response Jesus gave to the lukewarm
was anything but meek and mild,
reminding us if we warm but never burn
we are not fire! 12/20/23

Making the solstice personal.

Perhaps Today will be Your Solstice

Perhaps today you will stop in your tracks,
consider reversing direction. 12/21/23

Well, it wasn't quite that easy.

All You Have to Do to Get an A

A whimsical comment from one long ago
learning I was teaching a course in religion:
"All you have to do to get an A from Charlie
is to affirm the cosmos by sneezing." 12/21/23

Conscience is nothing
but the scrutiny of God
planted in our soul. 12/22/23

Claims to be Christian
are verified by actions
toward the least of these. 12/22/23

Believe it or not, there's something else to visit in Ripley.

Candle in a Window

Travelers through Ripley in southern Ohio
would do their souls good
to search out the Rankin House
on a high hill looking to Kentucky
where a candle in a window
signaled refuge on the journey
from Egypt to the Promised Land.
Come to an actual place
compassion made holy. 12/22/23

Sparked by a memory.

Walking the Via Dolorosa

In Jerusalem long ago
I walked the Via Dolorosa
trying to imagine that day.
Not one of us I now realize
needs to set out to travel
beyond the holy place where we live
to walk the Via Dolorosa. 12/22/23

Once again trying to imagine.

Hallowed by Anguish

I walked among olive trees
in Jerusalem long ago
where a man abandoned by his friends
is said to have begged his Father
to let the bitter cup pass,
dreading a hard night ahead
and a harder tomorrow.
Never will you forget it
if you've stood silent in a place
hallowed by anguish. 12/23/23

I doubt not I too would have fled.

I Can

Can you imagine
the shame of those scattering,
leaving him in all likelihood
to be killed? 12/23/23

I'd love to tell you the story behind this one.

Exchanges of gifts
between artist and poet—
crystalline moment. 12/23/23

If you make it to Madrid, don't for your soul's sake miss the Prado.

Goya caught it best—
Saturn consuming his son,
war's obscenity. 12/24/23

If we stop singing, war wins.

But We Must

It's hard to keep singing
peace on Earth, good will toward men
while bombs are obliterating. 12/24/23

*Victimhood, enflamed by a self-proclaimed savior—where does it
lead but the seeking of vengeance, and where does that lead but to
war?*

Beware the Savior

Does being victimized
give one justification
to turn the tables?
Beware the one promising salvation
by way of getting even. 12/24/23

A last meal together, that and more.

How can it not Seize the Imagination?

When in Italy years ago
I learned Leonardo was but one of many artists
who painted the last supper.
How can it not seize the imagination
to think of a master on his knees
washing as do servants the feet of his friends,
then entreating them to remember him
after their last meal together? 12/26/23

*Contrition, yet another word needing rehabilitation—when better
suited than at the beginning of a new year?*

If Resolutions Ever Succeed

"O my God, I am heartily sorry
for having offended Thee"—
so began what in my Catholic youth
was called the Act of Contrition.
Long years later I find myself pondering
these words that still arrest
as I look back on a year ending,
ahead to a year beginning,
wondering what have I done or failed to do
for which I am heartily sorry?
If resolutions ever succeed,
must they not stand upon contrition? 12/26/23

"Heartily sorry"
becomes singsong and ho-hum
until it strikes fire. 12/26/23

*When Mary Oliver said she had never missed the full moon, I bet
that included times when she couldn't see it.*

Full Moon

Due to cloud cover this evening,
I'll smile when looking up
to know what's hidden. 12/26/23

*See if the change of pronoun doesn't open up a whole different
feeling.*

Colossal Dream, Colossal Privilege

Before woodstove's flaming this morning
I find myself imagining God's dream
before she came up with light
which would morph eons later
into beings capable of returning her love.
What colossal privilege
to be one of those dreamed! 12/27/23

"Courtship" never loses its magic when its beginning is remembered.

Like a Brigand from the Bush

How do you expect me to remember
the topic of her presentation
when she had let her hair down,
was wearing a lovely blue dress,
and looked straight in my eyes and smiled?
I tell you May 14th of '75
will forever for me be the day
when destiny leapt like a brigand from the bush
to begin whirling me dervishly! 12/28/23

It felt important.

An Earnest Conversation

While waiting for the sun
on the last day of the year
my grandson of almost 8 and I chatted
about tucking into our hearts
the important people and dogs
who had crossed the Rainbow Bridge—
well now, that was an earnest conversation
I trust the two of us will long remember. 1/1/24

We all blow it at times when disciplining a child. Can we acknowledge it, resolving to do better?

Opportunity at Hand for Healing

Think of the gift
for a child to hear from a stand-in for God,
"You didn't deserve that.
I'm sorry I lost perspective.
I can do better." 1/1/24

Would that we remember the resources we have at hand.

Shh, Just Lean in to Listen

Imagine sitting in the presence
of one living or dead
who has so touched your heart,
calmed your fear
or fired your spirit
as to come to embody for you
both comfort and wisdom.
Imagine this oasis in your desert
has invited you at this juncture in your journey
to close your eyes,
open your heart,
and just listen.
What good, you protest, this idle game?
Shh, just imagine,
then lean in to listen. 1/2/24

A grandmother's good reason for taking a risk.

Of Course it's Worth Taking

Progressive loss of vision in one eye
has necessitated later today
a corneal transplant for my Penny—
a risky proposition with no guarantees
but of course it's worth taking
because soon taking your grandkids to Disney World,
don't you do all you can
to see better? 1/2/24

Surgery day.

It Goes with the Territory.

Right now she's under the knife—
well, only the eye getting the transplant
but still the knife.
And knowing her history of allergic reactions
makes the risk feel more than academic.
We're talking here the love of my life
so indulge me a little with my worry.
It goes with the territory
when your heart has been tamed.
She'd worry too were it happening to me—
it's the same territory. 1/2/24

It's hard to take stock without slowing down.

Stepping Back from the Flow

⟲

Think of meditation or prayer
as stepping back from the flow
long enough to decide if you're content
with being carried willy-nilly downstream
or whether instead it's time to row. 1/4/24

"Blessed are the peacemakers"—Jesus was nothing if not radically courageous.

Shot at from Both Directions

⟲

Peacemaking is not for the faint of heart.
For refusing to take sides
intent only on killing's cessation,
you catch flak from both directions
for giving comfort to the enemy. 1/4/24

Friends are not simply there to comfort.

Unsolicited Truth from Faithful Friends

⟲

Let's hear it for the courage of friends
willing to stop us in our tracks
when observing behavior that offends.
Think how many in the world
only change course with the help
of unsolicited truth from faithful friends. 1/4/24

Can healing and reconciliation be possible if the cause of the division is ignored?

Appomattox did not End the Civil War

That grievances last for centuries
sickening succeeding generations
speaks to the power of family dynamics—
not thinking nuclear family here
but national.
Appomattox did not end the Civil War
soon eulogized as a noble lost cause,
slavery ignored. 1/4/24

A thought when greeted by a new morning.

When You're Benevolent Today

Benevolence rises from the maelstrom
across billions of years.
Think when you're benevolent today
you're advancing creation! 1/4/24

Just think about who never will be dislodged from your heart.

Once Magic Happens in the Heart

The thing about timeless moments
is they're unthreatened by time's passing.
Once magic happens in the heart,
is it not held there forever? 1/5/24

A plea to sidestep the question, "Which is your favorite?"

Be like a Neophyte in a Museum

It's a mean game the intellect likes to play
deciding among attractions which is one's favorite.
Once the winner is determined,
will not the others by the comparison seem diminished?
Instead be like a neophyte in a museum
with absolutely no expectation—
exhilarated before each painting
finding favorite after favorite! 1/5/23

Shifting the context elevates the meaning.

Peaceful Transfer of Power

Having used the phrase in a poem
referring to current events
I received a felicitous response
from a friend who opened it wider.
In the quiet of your heart
put yourself in the presence
of one who has ignited in you
either wisdom or courage
and then be awed to experience
a peaceful transfer of power! 1/6/24

Keep this in mind next time you read a poem or view a painting.

Though Brief Epic Deep

A poem's like a painting in a museum.
Rushing past one to take in the next
risks skimming the story.
Doubtless lacking the novel's panorama,
the story in a poem or a painting
though brief aims epic deep. 1/5/24

Citizens of the future will look back in disbelief.

Before You Cast Your Vote

A question before you cast your vote
in the upcoming momentous election:
Do you realize if it's for the former guy
that the twelve hundred convicted
for trashing the Capitol (intending even worse)
at the bidding on their inciter in chief
too ashamed to accept defeat
will not only be pardoned and championed
but replaced by those who had the patriotism
to put them there?
Vindictive without relief
was and still is the inciter-in-chief
who believe it or not is seeking re-election.
Please don't be deceived by disinformation
(euphemism for outright lies)
before you cast your vote. 1/6/24

Lacrimae rerum, unforgettable phrase from Virgil's The Aenid.

Included in the Tears of Things

I'm guessing Virgil included
when writing of the tears of things
the pain inflicted by words
that can't be taken back. 1/6/24

Fearing losing face
ego finds this the hardest—
begging forgiveness. 1/6/24

Remembering Job, the following is perhaps not outrageous.

Forgiving Reality and God

A gem from Richard Rohr:
"The only way out of dualism
is a universal forgiveness of reality
for being what it is."
Perhaps what this brings us to
is the brink of revelation:
God too needs forgiving! 1/9/24

If there is remorse for having hurt, there is hope.

Things That Will Not Go Unremembered

When you are aggrieved to realize
words from your lips or your pen have wounded,
cannot be taken back,
will not go unremembered,
do not despair.
Has not everyone in the world
hurled in furious moments
their most callous or thoughtless?
Regret heartfully felt then expressed
with resolve to be more mindful,
that too will not go unremembered,
in fact is very likely
to carry longer. 1/9/24

Instant replays can be excruciating.

Dagger of Light

How could I,
how could I,
how could I?
But I did.
Dagger of light. 1/10/24

The quotations in what follows are from Harriet Beecher Stowe and Frederick Douglass.

Should not to Biden Go the Credit?

Seeing Biden catch it
from the left as well as the right
calls to mind Lincoln.
"Lincoln is a strong man,
but his strength is of a peculiar kind.
It is the strength not so much of a stone buttress
as of a wire cable.
It is a strength swaying to every influence,
yielding on this side and on that to popular needs,
yet tenaciously and inflexibly bound
to carry its great end..."
"Reproaches came thick and fast upon him
from within and from without,
and from opposite quarters.
He was assailed by abolitionists;
he was assailed by slaveholders..."
If to Lincoln went the credit
for saving the Union,
should not to Biden go the credit
if for at least the past three-plus years
what's being saved is democracy? 1/10/24

Scientists keep warning but what hope when politicians are beholden to the fossil fuel industry?

2023 Burning

How many hottest years on record will it take?
Mississippi burning was bad enough
but that pale dot in the heavens we call home
is *now* what's burning. 1/10/24

Wonderment Unending

Does not the great variety
of humankind's names for the divine
attest to wonderment unending
before the greatest of all mysteries? 1/11/24

It is hard for the privileged even to imagine the destitute.

Crust in the Gutter

What if a crust in the gutter
was all you had to nibble
until lucky enough to find another
or else beg from a passing brother? 1/11/24

Take some time with this one.

Become Today Luther

Become today Luther.
What exactly is it
you would post for all to see
declaring "Here I stand,
I can do no other!"? 1/11/24

Remembering a musician beloved friend.

I Swear She's Right There with Me

I'm savoring her presence,
my friend who seemed to have left us
four years ago this day.
Absence, where is your sting
if friendship lasts forever?
When music lifts me up,
starts carrying me away,
I swear she's right there with me. 1/12/24

You're telling me a God of love lacks capacity to feel?

God's Sorrow

How can God be indifferent
when her children spew hate? 1/12/24

Are odds not astronomical against any one of us meeting, much less arcing fire toward the miracle of that interstellar wonder we call friendship?

Wildest of Flukes Meant to Be

Thinking of eight billion human vibrancies
taking in breath this very moment,
the odds against any two intersecting
(much less arcing fire
in that miracle we call friendship)
are beyond astronomical
which means having you in my life
feels like winning the jackpot—
wildest of flukes it logically would seem
but doesn't it nonetheless feel
like it was meant to be? 1/12/24

No forgiveness without empathy.

Take a Deep Dive into Empathy

When you next catch yourself saying
that's something I could never forgive,
take a deep dive into empathy
until humbled and elated
you find yourself realizing
of course you can forgive. 1/13/24

Prompted by Pascal.

What Words Would You Sew into Your Coat?

The woodstove blaze this morning
calls to mind Pascal's words
sewn into his coat so he'd never forget
an experience seared into his soul.
"Since about half-past ten in the evening
until about half-past midnight,
FIRE. Certitude. Certitude. Feeling. Joy. Peace."
Doesn't it make you wonder
looking back on your life
what words you would sew into your coat
to help you remember for the rest of your days
an experience seared into your soul? 1/14/24

Something to ponder when fear comes knocking.

How Cope with Fear?

How cope with fear?
Comfort another afraid.
Friendship means vastly more
than partying together.
Think lighthouse beacon,
rock in storm,
arm to hold tight to.
When skies again brighten,
time to party then! 1/16/24

In defense of preaching to the choir.

Whom Better to Preach To?

Whom better to preach to than the choir
if they're to find heart to keep singing. 1/16/24

Pay attention when wisdom figures are in sync. The Hopkins reference in what follows is to his poem "God's Grandeur."

Buddha, Jesus and Hopkins

Ancient fear leaps from the shadows
with each fresh provocation.
Are they crazy then, Buddha and Jesus,
when they counsel us not to fear
or are they reminding us of the faith
they share with the poet Hopkins?
"Oh, morning, at the brown brink eastward springs
because the Holy Ghost over the bent world broods
with warm breast and with ah! bright wings." 1/16/24

What colossal achievement of the universe: conscience!

The Magnitude of Having a Conscience

You may call it a burden,
I call it both privilege and calling—
the magnitude of having a conscience? 1/16/24

If you thought she was childless, think again.

Her Children will Carry Her Forward

Can it really be
she's been gone now five years?
I beam knowing Mary Oliver's children
like me will carry her forward. 1/17/24

Mary Oliver Saluting Her Brother Walt Whitman

Mary gives a clue here
into why she considered Walt Whitman
the brother she never had.
"But first and foremost, I learned from Whitman
that the poem is a temple—
or a green field."
Learning the deep affinity
one beloved poet has for another,
does it not prompt a return to their temples,
to the green fields each created? 1/16/24

The best antidote I can think of.

Bring Today Someone Comfort

It can consume you if you let it,
the suffering of the world.
Bring today somebody comfort. 1/17/24

I mean, doesn't it stand to reason?

Please, Mr. Scientist

Can nature be impersonal
if she has given birth to persons?
Please, Mr. Scientist,
use your reason. 1/17/24

Remembering back to the 60s.

Standing on their Shoulders

We stand on the shoulders
of those facing odds we can't imagine—
never losing heart, ever soldiering on
toward the justice of their dream.
May we ride the wave of their vision and courage.
"We shall overcome!" 1/17/24

Think of the power of a glacier, then realize we can add to one!

Justice like a Glacier

It takes generations beyond decades
but justice like a glacier
relentlessly is on the move—
can anything match the dignity of being part
of an immense steady flow
grinding injustice down? 1/17/24

Quality time, when you think about it, is a luminous pulsing phrase.

Quality Time Together

What a world of difference
between passing time with someone
with whom you're occupying the same space
and spending quality time
with someone upon whom you choose
to lavish your attention.
Words need not be spoken
but presence, guaranteed, will be remembered. 1/18/24

Another instance of the Greeks paving the way.

Chronos and Kairos

Chronos and kairos—
two Greek words for telling time
reminding that the tick of the clock
is the far less important kind.
Play time,
heart-touching time,
time beyond time
when gasping ah! before beauty,
communion time—
moments forever remembered
have nothing to do with the watch on your wrist
measuring tock after tick. 1/18/24

Guess who wants quality time with you?

Prayer as Quality Time

Think of prayer
as spending quality time with God
(or whatever name you give Great Mystery)
eager, if you can believe it,
to spend quality time with you. 1/18/24

Forty-five years ago to the day, she perished in a fire.

A Supernova Named Josine

Remembering Sun and Earth only exist
because of the explosive generosity of a dying star,
I'm holding converse this morning
with a supernova named Josine
who departed in flames long ago,
her generosity seeding mine
among many heavens. 1/20/24

Let the image invite revelation.

Poet's Query

How many things today
can your eyes find to kiss? 1/22/24

Measuring stick for an enlivening encounter.

A Breath of Fresh Air

An encounter is enlivening
if each ponders upon leaving,
"Now that was a breath of fresh air." 1/21/24

If soil is packed hard
even seeds packed with promise
hardly have a prayer. 1/21/24

Yearn brings hope down to Earth.

There's Something about Yearn

"What do you hope for?"
likely will prompt abstractions
like "peace and prosperity."
"What do you yearn for so strongly
it feels deeper than an ache?"
likely will dispel an inclination
to wander into abstraction. 1/22/24

Emily Dickinson's answer to regret: "I dwell in possibility."

How to Stop Feeding Regret

Dwelling each day in possibility
effectively stops feeding regret. 1/22/24

Rather than finally being reunited, were they ever really apart?

Can There Really have been Separation?

On the surface it would seem
he's had to live without her
since her final departure years prior,
but can there really have been separation
for two bound in the heart? 1/23/24

Hearts bound remember—
whatever then may befall,
two stand together. 1/23/24

We're kin if this resonates.

Why Search for Another Vein?

What is it about me
when I finish a book touching my heart,
expanding my mind,
or stirring my soul
(or wondrously all three!)
that instead of searching for a new one
I want right away to reread it
to kindle further a flame
I can only call holy.
Why search for another vein
having just struck gold? 1/25/24

Sneezes unpoetic? I beg to differ.

In Praise of the Involuntary

I think what I find so satisfying
in an explosive sneeze
is its involuntary nature.
Rising from nowhere it carries me with it
reminding of the mystery we called Spirit
blowing when and where it will. 1/25/24

It's good for the heart—
trusting those we bid farewell
rest now with their friends. 1/25/24

If we're to become like unto them, mustn't it involve play?

Poised for Play

Poised for play—
along with their wonderment at the world
and their eagerness to exchange affection,
isn't that what they teach us,
the little children? 1/25/24

Grandparenthood is a trip.

No Mountain could Echo Farther

I'll tell you what's great—
to wake up one morning
and to know that you're eight!
And if you a grandparent of this boy,
no mountain could echo farther
the shout of your joy. 1/26/24

The rest of your life
some words you'll remember
for cutting so deep. 1/26/24

Wren's late January gift.

Mustn't We Sing When We Can?

A sudden warm morning
after weeks of deep cold
brings from Wren a bright song.
Shivering he must have been waiting.
Too soon, it's still winter,
I could cry out but I won't.
Mustn't we sing when we can? 1/26/24

If you make it to elderhood, may you be blessed to savor the wealth of a journey punctuated with priceless friends.

A New Kind of Mass

Banter galore but so much more
when old guys gather monthly
to spark each other's memories
of remarkable life journeys
compounded now in interest and joy
by golden friendship.
A Catholic onlooker would be excused
in surmising these old guys bantering
must be celebrating a new kind of Mass
beginning with remembrance,
ending with Communion. 1/26/24

Feel blessed when you experience what makes the universe run.

When Smitten

Searching for words when smitten
is of course futile
but don't we have to try
so others at least catch a hint
of what makes the universe run?
Have we not entered the precinct of the holy,
the realm of the ineffable,
when the best we can manage is a stammer
after the grace of being smitten? 1/27/24

The characters are from Marilynne Robinson's Jack, one of her Gilead novels.

Throwing Caution to the Wind

It's unfathomable why innocent Della
would throw caution to the wind
for the likes of pitiable Jack
unless we take her at her word
that she saw into his soul.
Can you think of a better reason
to throw caution to the wind? 1/29/24

Namaste.

Face to Face

Pondering the face of God
I catch glimmers wherever my glance falls,
whoever my path crosses,
even (my God!) when I look into the mirror.
Could it be we don't have to wait
to see face to face? 1/29/24

On the open journey don't we carry each other?

How Can They be Gone

Two vital to my life breathed their last
on this day years apart.
How can they be gone
if they're still in my heart? 1/30/24

Here I look back on a day in my life when I was reminded of the power of words.

It Should Come as No Surprise

There I was in the Dickens Museum—
struck by the power of words on a page
that had affected my life deeply—
with a young woman companion
with whom I had recently spoken words
decisive in our relationship.
So it should come as no surprise
why I'm remembering fifty-one years later
the life-changing importance
of words written and spoken
in old London town 1/29/24

My candidate for the richest day of the month.

Grateful Harvest, Giddy Anticipation

My candidate for richest day of the month?
The very last
when we look back on thirty days of bounty,
harvest new advances in understanding,
then giddily anticipate on the morrow
a new lottery won! 1/31/24

Light is not always either welcome or soothing. Thank goodness!

Another Angle on Light

What chance does truth have
when minds are closed like steel traps,
hearts hard as cold marble?
None until a dagger of light
pierces to the rescue. 1/31/24

Once on the ballot, is not each alternative grim?

Pray God the Nation Comes to its Senses

If he succeeds in getting on the ballot
can anyone honestly imagine
he'll accept defeat next time around
regardless the count of the votes?
Of course he'll again insist it was stolen
and what are his armed patriots to do
but refuse to take it!
As grim as this prospect if he loses,
grimmer would be the military state to follow
should this champion of autocracy win.
Pray God the nation comes to its senses
and keeps him off the ballot.
Otherwise either alternative is grim. 1/31/24

Who am I, in case you wonder.

Call Me a Poet

Teacher, preacher,
reacher, breacher—
call me a poet,
wild child of the universe
grateful just to be here
and needing to sing
from my heart and my soul
of the stupendous beauty of it all. 2/1/24

Groundhog Day, cause for recollection.

Groundhog and Human Heart

Halfway point
between solstice and equinox—
Candlemas they called it,
Imbolc further back
honoring groundhog and human heart
each emerging from cold shadow,
dreaming warm sun. 2/1/24

Not a parent alive will not understand this one.

Wintered Hearts Singing

For our daughter
resplendent beyond reach of pale words
to have arrived in our arms
at the halfway point between winter

and soon to awaken spring,
well, let's just say February First
will forever make the wintered hearts
of two parents I know sing. 2/1/24

But other things, too, mark February 1st as a day that stands out.

Wildly Divergent Feelings

First sit-in in Greensboro,
Challenger exploding in thin air,
daughter first placed in our arms—
is there any wonder
at our wildly divergent feelings
each year at this exact midpoint
between winter and spring? 2/1/24

Valor calls to mind battle. Here's one to match any.

Venom and Valor

Imagine if you can
sitting at a Greensboro lunch counter
to protest your Jim Crow exclusion
with taunts screamed in your ears,
ketchup poured over your head,
and not raising a finger
except for the might of your presence.
Vivid may it remain in America's memory,
a day of venom and valor. 2/1/24

There's an exhibit that helps with the imagining.

Education not Found in a Book

There's a museum exhibit in Atlanta
where you brace to place your hands
on a counter as it literally begins shaking
while through earphones you shudder to listen
to shrieks threatening your life
as ketchup decorates your hair.
It leaves you wondering
not only where they found the faith
but the courage. 2/1/24

Cairn signals story, stop and imagine.

Announcing Something Here Happened

When you find as you walk in the woods
stones stacked upon stones
you recognize something here happened
worthy of remembrance.
If your heart inclines you to linger,
you just might find yourself adding
a stone of your own to deepen
the hush in the woods. 2/1/24

Resurrection takes folks in different directions.

Just What She Wanted it to Mean

Lines from Marilynne Robinson's Lila
speak a kind of truth on resurrection,
that will be convincing neither to skeptics nor dogmatists
but perhaps more important for all that.
"She understood the word resurrection
to mean just what she wanted it to mean.
The idea was precious to her—
Doll just the way she used to be
but with death behind her
and all the peace that would come with that.
Doll would laugh at the surprise of it all."
Just imagine one loved and lost
resurrected like that. 2/1/24

Imagine with me John Lennon singing, Give empathy a chance.

America's Long Ago Sin

You who scoff
to hear talk of America's original sin,
doubtless the hue of your skin
is neither red nor black.
Empathy, granted, is the hardest thing
but mustn't we at least try? 2/1/24

Sometimes shattering words are what it takes.

It was Time Once Again to Leave Home

Fifty-five years ago today
at a point where my life felt careening
I had to escape for weeks
Chicago's cold for Mobile's warmth.
Piercing words from a friend
the night before my flight south
had suddenly not only unlocked a door
but thrown it wide open.
The Jesuits had been home for a decade
but in a flash it became clear
that for the second time in my life
it was time to leave home. 2/4/24

A new lease on life—
cliché but isn't it true,
waking each morning? 2/6/24

Looking back for a clue prior to my bidding the church of my youth adieu.

No Greater Bane

On a long ago evening in Ireland
while watching a program on Islam
like a dagger of light it pierced home
how is this path not as valid as mine?
Is there anything more demeaning
than an exclusivist's claim
when it comes to possessing truth? 2/6/24

There's a long story behind this one, but others might fill in the gaps, remembering a mysterium quid of their own that they finally had to stand up to, or might now be ready to.

My Nemesis was a Phantom

For years I felt jinxed
by a mysterious something
relating to certain symptom reoccurrence
that I simply called "mysterium quid"
until forty-seven years ago today
I refused to give in and suddenly realized
my nemesis was a phantom! 2/6/24

Imagine sitting in your own.

Council of Eagles—
each recounting flights soaring
in the high thermals! 2/6/24

A harder imagining.

⌒

Imagine Jesus
after being gassed at Auschwitz
tossed in an oven. 2/7/24

What else are you here for?

Your Own Life Stands Witness

⌒

Be wary of exclusivist claims
when it comes to the truth.
Is not the door of the universe
ever open to new emergence?
Ride the great wave forward
convinced not only that the story isn't over
but that your own life stands witness
to new truth emerging.
Create something today—
a kindness, a courage—
never before seen
in the history of the cosmos! 2/8/24

Yet another arena where dogmatists are terrified of freedom.

A Say in the Matter

Before you weigh in
with your fervent good reasons
why assisted suicide for the terminally ill
(more accurately called death with dignity)
is a sin against the Holy Spirit,
would you yourself in dire circumstances
not like a say in the matter? 2/7/24

The documentary was entitled Last Flight Home.

Responses Born of Witness

Some spoke of courage,
others of power,
still others of a deep sense of calm
and praise for purposefulness and preparation—
all comforting with compassion one terminally ill
profoundly grateful for the respect
accorded his clear declaration
that it was time to rest free of suffering,
time to board in peace and in trust
the last flight home. 2/8/24

Being reminded why I write.

Goosebump Confirmation

When someone responds
to a poem I have written
saying what it brought were goosebumps,
I'm confirmed in what feels my calling.
I aim less for the mind than something deeper.
Goosebumps always announce
what I have written has landed! 2/8/24

Remembering a church talk I gave on this day long ago, this was the crux.

What Three Words, Spirit Journeyer?

Think of composing an oath of honor
condensed into three words
as a pledge from your deep spirit
to be repeated each morning.
What three words, spirit journeyer,
belong in your oath? 2/8/24

Deep hate and deep love—
cavernous the human heart
capable of both. 2/9/24

An invitation to remember what it felt like to be wooed, and then to imagine.

God is on the Make

Scott Peck used to shock audiences
when he'd proclaim that God is on the make.
Let it stop your heart after blowing your mind
to imagine being wooed by nothing less
than the force animating the sweep of the universe
in love's direction. 2/9/24

Books are babies too. This one will be entitled Glimmerings and Stammerings.

Finishing touches
on my new gift to the world—
such joy to give birth! 2/9/24

That Crazy Horse had powerful experiences there prompted me to pick up a stone on my climb to the summit.

Power Stone Invites Dreams

A vision quest stone
from my ascent to Bear Butte
each night invites dreams. 2/9/24

John Steinbeck sowed the seed when writing of his "Welsh rats"
who niggled away at him with worries, unassailable until he named
them.

Create Your Own Mythology

Let mythology live for you.
Open your eyes to the jostling
of the inhabitants of your inner world.
Consider creating a name
for each vying for attention—
be assured there are many.
One thwarts your advance?
Call then upon another.
What resources, what drama! 2/10/24

A felicitous inspiration, then suddenly a rainbow—idle coincidence?

Epiphany in Sligo

A leading in Ireland long ago
after an illumination in Steinbeck:
why not create my own mythology?
Then a synchronicity
while hitching south of Sligo —
a rainbow! 2/10/24

How can it end well
when one party's candidate
can't accept defeat? 2/9/24

Movies can be great, but nothing quite grips like live theater.

On Theater and Therapy

It happened again.
Last year it was a playhouse in Bedford
where 12 Angry Men blew me away.
Yesterday it was a playhouse in Roanoke
where this time it was The Mountaintop,
the evening before Martin was blown away.
Theater is therapy as ancient Greeks knew
cleansing by way of catharsis
our deepest fear and pity.
Brace yourselves when you next head to a theater.
The best therapy session of your life
just might be lying in wait
to blow you away. 2/11/24

Dialogue at the Lorraine Motel: far more riveting than any Superbowl.

Infinitely More Important

Smack dab in the middle
of all the Super Bowl hoopla
we went to see The Mountaintop
and were shaken to our souls to be reminded
of something infinitely more important. 2/11/24

Imagine if we stopped thinking of the universe as an "it."

What's with Calling Her "That"?

Which is more astounding
when thinking of the universe—
we're a part of all that
or all that is a part of us?
And if we clearly are persons,
what's with calling this mother that birthed us
a "that"? 2/11/24

Jonathan Eig's new biography of MLK gives a deeper glimpse.

Vessel of Clay

Is the high reach of King's achievement—
think the lasting effect of his vision and his courage!—
tarnished by his infidelities?
Does it not depend
on whether one's focus is on the vessel
or the elixir that poured from it?
Likely the envy of the angels
is not that stardust has become clay
but that clay with its evident flaws
has the capacity with enough vision and courage
to become a vessel! 2/10/24

Nondescript day? it doesn't have to be.

Morning Query

Magnificent meaning "making great,"
think by what act of kindness or courage
you might make today magnificent. 2/11/24

*Liza Field is her name—her monthly Earth column in Roanoke's
paper was little short of magic.*

Words from a Spirit Kin

The only time I met her in person
was twelve years ago this evening
when she inspired all listening
(as for years she's done with her writing)
with her felt kinship with all things wild
beginning with the mountains!
Amazing how words from a spirit kin
whether written or spoken
not only unite but ignite! 2/10/24

*I mean, it's a day about love, is it not? And if you have trouble with
the pronoun, think about correcting an imbalance.*

February 14th

On your Valentine's card to God today,
what would you say?
Look all around
to find hers to you. 2/13/24

Playacting sounds frivolous until the curtain rises.

Partitions Disappear

Acting is a calling—
empathy so far-reaching,
impersonation so authentic,
that partitions disappear
not only between actor and role
but between audience and actor! 2/12/24

Valentine's Day 1973—a kiss coming to you in whimsy.

Don't Miss the Wink in Me Eye

Long ago in Cork, Ireland
I kissed the famed stone in Blarney Castle
(upside down would you believe
as lips could reach it in no other way)
on Valentine's of all days,
so take with grain of salt or dram of Guinness
everything emanating from my mouth
on every subject but wild love ever since,
missing not in the process
the wink in a leprechaun's eye
reminding you of your own wild love
coexistent with your own not insubstantial
capacity for sheer blarney. 2/13/24

From King Lear, Act 5, Scene 3. Spend a month with this one.

Reason Alone to Call the Bard Eternal

Have more poignant words
ever been sung by human tongue
than Lear coming out of madness
singing to his sweet Cordelia
cast down thinking of her false sisters?
"No, no, no, no. Come, let's away to prison.
We two alone will sing like birds i'th' cage.
When thou dost ask me blessing, I'll kneel down
And ask of thee forgiveness. So we'll live,
And pray, and sing, and tell old tales, and laugh
At gilded butterflies, and hear poor rogues
Talk of court news, and we'll talk with them too—
Who loses and who wins; who's in, who's out—
And take upon 's the mystery of things,
As if we were God's spies. And we'll wear out,
In a walled prison, packs and sects of great ones
That ebb and flow by th' moon."
Would we not,
had he written nothing else,
call the bard eternal? 2/13/24

Breath, wind and spirit—
ponder the immensity
of the overlap! 2/13/24

The quote is from The Blessed Virgin Compared to the Air We Breathe by Gerard Manley Hopkins, poet-priest extraordinaire.

May We Feast While We Still Can

Ever since we emerged from the womb
have we not been catching our breath?
Sink with Hopkins into the wonder of it.
"My more than meat and drink,
my meal at every wink!"
May we feast while we still can
on the airy banquet spread before us. 2/13/24

This didn't pan out, but it was a not implausible possibility.

Nikki Haley is No Dummy

Nikki Haley is no dummy.
Why not hang in there
no matter how far behind
when the only one ahead of you
not improbably will implode
by the weight of the evidence
of his mendacity and corruption.
Does not someone need to be ready
to step into the breach?
Whatever one's views of her,
at least she threatens not democracy. 2/13/24

Pondering a recurring question.

Pulsing Right Here

But one of the problems with the question
"Do you believe in God?"
is it makes it sound like God
(if believed in)
is not only separate
but somewhere out there looking in
rather than pulsing right here looking out. 2/14/24

Continuing the rumination with, perhaps, a surprising wish.

I Wish You Many Gods

I wish you many gods.
Jealous of each other you imagine?
You've got to be kidding.
Think of them swirling as they dance
shouting to you on the sidelines
to leave behind your analytical mind
and for God's sake (and your own)
join in the only Dance there is! 2/14/24

Proselytizers
only listen to refute,
have an agenda. 2/15/24

Smile to remember
you have all the time you need.
Float like a feather. 2/15/24

Has not Trump long since
been unleashing dogs of war
by fueling hatred? 2/17/24

Ever Wonder Why Lemmings Leap?

What do lemmings fear more than death?
Admitting they've been hoodwinked. 2/17/24

The history is not distant.

Think Hitler and Sudentenland

Do you really believe Putin
will stop with Ukraine?
Think Hitler and Sudentenland in thirty-eight
while the West was saying let's wait. 2/17/24

Hanging with pacifists forces deep questions.

Or Simply a Fool Risking All?

Is a pacifist a coward
leaving the dirty work to others
or simply a fool risking all
for the sake of a vision?
Might it exact even more
to make peace instead of war?
Didn't Buddha and Jesus make clear
where they stood on the subject,
Gandhi and King too? 2/17/24

No wonder he's banking all on getting reelected.

An Upheaval Lies Up Ahead

The only thing that will keep Trump
from ending up in prison
is getting reelected.
Should that fail again,
his fervent prayer (if he prays for anything)
is that his carefully groomed Brown Shirts
will never permit it.
Is it not guaranteed
an upheaval lies up ahead
unless (worst case scenario)
he get's reelected instead? 2/17/24

Balero's slow building to a crescendo is layered for me with meaning.

Somehow Balero Marked It

Fifty-one years ago this morning
I listened to Ravel's Balero
building to its thrilling crescendo
unaware that by evening
I would be standing on the other side
of what I have come to call
the Great Divide of my life—
Catholicism behind,
ahead who knew what.
Somehow Balero marked it
with its thrilling thrust to a crescendo. 2/18/24

Realize with Zeus
you have in your arsenal
lightning bolts to hurl. 2/18/24

Fair Aphrodite,
think wild impulse to create—
exult to be her! 2/18/24

Faithful Hestia
devotee to hearth and home,
tending to the fire. 2/18/24

Welcome Artemis—
virgin goddess like Mary—
into your free heart. 2/18/24

Think of Hephaestus
blazing away at his forge,
always creating. 2/18/24

Poets, naïve or far-seeing—in either event they love nothing more than Earth.

Mary Oliver's Credo

"I believe everything has a soul."
O these poets,
what children! 2/18/24

Dear God, not again at the helm.

Response to Blatant Murder

When one's response to blatant murder
clearly ordered from Moscow
is "America kills people too,"
your soul has been exposed,
or lack thereof. 2/19/24

There I go getting political again, but don't we all live in a polis and is not the polis at risk?

Nightmare Ticket

Don't count it out,
nightmare ticket to gaze upon aghast—
Donald Trump and Jim Jordan,
or long shot Tucker Carlson. 2/19/24

Kisses colliding—
just one of our rituals
when Penny walks by. 2/19/24

A lapdog can carry you all the way back.

Thrumming Ever Since

Buckley is so positioned on my lap
that I feel his heart thrumming
reminding me of my own heart
long ago beginning its own thrumming
in blissful confinement
in the womb of my mother. 2/19/24

Doesn't rereading make sense if the right chord has been struck?

Instead of Reaching for a New Book

Instead of reaching for a new book
upon ending one that struck a deep chord
I find myself beginning all over
to search out again that chord.
Why not keep returning
to something that carried you away? 2/19/24

Unquenchable flame
is buried in Russian hearts—
Navalny's not dead! 2/19/24

First he trashed Hillary,
now he is trashing Biden.
Donald the Trasher. 2/19/24

Who doesn't love a good story?

Somebody Tell a Story

When things get too cerebral,
come back down to Earth.
Somebody tell a story! 2/19/24

Never tune out a retelling.

Every Story is Layered

Heard a story before
and inclined to tune it out?
Listen for a new layer. 2/19/24

Pondering immortality here.

Get Serious—He Still Lives

Can Dvorak be but a name on a page,
mere cipher reminiscent
of a presence long gone,
when today he lifted me to high heaven?
Get serious—he still lives! 2/19/24

It's all in how you ask the question.

The Difference between Hope and Yearning

Tell me what you hope for
and I'll hear from your mind.
Tell me what you yearn for with aching
and I'll not only glimpse your soul
but know you better. 2/20/24

William James nailed it.

Expulsive Power of New Love

Ultimately we transcend grieving
not by forgetting a love's passing
(not possible)
but, in William James' wise words,
by the expulsive power of a new love to come.
No hurry here
for first we have to heave
the world of our sorrow into what feels
an emptiness that devours,
but if we keep open our heart
someone or something in the fullness of time
will come with its expulsive power
to surprise us with new love. 2/20/24

Doesn't finding a cairn stir something deep?

Reverently Adding a Stone

Think the reverence
behind adding a stone
to a cairn you discover
in a walk through the woods
knowing you're sanctifying further
ground that is holy. 2/20/24

Is not each foray into silence the crossing of a threshold into both presence and possibility?

Temple of Silence

Enter silence as you would an ancient temple.
Does Presence ever fail
to invite not only reverence
but keen attention to the possibility
of revelation? 2/20/24

Any fastened to the heart of one with an ominous diagnosis will comprehend this one.

Non-Aggressive!

The word leapt from the page
to his immense relief—
the activity discerned in the testing
is pronounced "non-aggressive."
Immense relief as well
for those fastened to his heart
whether by blood or by spirit. 2/20/24

Isn't a secret belief in immortality at the heart of each creation?

Embers Left on Pages

Some day the burnt-out log of me
will duly be declared spent
but embers left on pages
will still warm with the fire of me. 2/21/24

Breathing lies at the core.

Each Next Breath Coming

It keeps coming, my next breath,
and I'm not even trying,
nor are eight billion across Earth,
sisters and brothers all,
breathing (or being breathed by)
each next breath coming. 2/21/24

Van Gogh's old man with his face in his hands—few paintings move me more.

When My Heart Goes Out

My heart goes out
when one buries her face in her hands
or another covers his face with his hands.
Words are not needed
to communicate despair. 2/21/24

Invite your ancestors to the next sunrise.

Imagine Your Ancestors through You Yearning

Have you ever gazed in wonder
at the Eastern horizon
knowing any instant it will tip fire?
Imagine your ancestors through you yearning
before it to bow again! 2/21/24

An attempt to broaden "erotic."

Erotic Universe

Can't you feel the pulsing,
the cacajada of creation,
being ever pulsing to be more?
Scott Peck perhaps came closest
when astonishing audiences
by proclaiming God is on the make! 2/21/24

You can't kill the dream.

Inextinguishable Their Fire

Navalny's assassination
calls back Lincoln's and King's—
unquenchable their fire,
irrepressible their dream.
The universe is so arranged that assassins
never have the last word. 2/21/24

The passage is from Mary Oliver's Blue Pastures.

The Awful Prison of Himself

"He sat back in the awful prison of himself"—
this from Mary Oliver about her abusive father
draws my mind like a magnet to a politician
seeming to enjoy disdaining many.
How not dwell in an awful prison
needing to disdain many? 2/22/24

A variation of the following—who's the easiest to identify with, and the hardest?

When Heading to the Theater

Here's a question to ponder
as you're next heading to the theater.
See if you can recognize a dimension of yourself
in each character about to strut
across the screen or the stage.
Think of it as an opportunity
to spy the variety of your disguises
in the never-failing suspense
of your strut across the stage. 2/21/24

Don't you hope your favorite authors are keeping at it?

New Revelations on the Way

What pleases me as I work on a new book
is thinking of favorite authors—
the list is long but for starters
are Robin Kimmerer, Sue Monk Kidd, Brian Swimme
    and Barbara Kingsolver—
working away at *their* new books.
Thinking of your *own* favorite authors,
don't you love to anticipate
new revelations on the way? 2/21/24

On the anniversary of my grandmother's passing.

On Longevity

Those of us hoping to live long
(I suspect that excludes no one
unless pain or sorrow overwhelms)
might remember that good health
will be essential if to enjoy it
and even then there are limits
as my grandmother in good health
expressed upon reaching 100,
"I wish I could just go to sleep
and not wake."
I'm reminded of Martin's words
about longevity being desirable
but there are more important things.
Grandmother made it to 105
before her wish was granted.
Thirty-three years ago today
I have to believe she was pleased
not to awaken. 2/22/24

Of Course Misery Loves Company

Of course misery loves company—
who wants to suffer alone? 2/23/24

Why it makes a difference is beyond explaining.

The Exact Time of the Full Moon

It will appear to some this evening
to others tomorrow evening
that the full moon is once again here
but actually its exact arrival
will be 7:30 tomorrow morning.
Some find pleasure in knowing
not only the day
but the hour and minute. 2/22/24

This one is for Marian.

More than Blood Cousins

It so happened
that at the funeral Mass of our grandmother
a bond with my cousin was forged
that we have come to know in our bones
(which is to say in our hearts)
is indestructible.
We both rose to the occasion
to offer words which of course fell short
of adequate expression of the collective grief
at the passing of our beloved grandmother
but which announced to each other
of a bond beyond blood.
I have to believe Grandmother looks down
and cheers the bond that keeps deepening
between more than blood cousins. 2/22/24

It's enough to look down on a name.

Knitting Needle Pen

Letters knit together
by the needle of a pen
into a velvety smooth name
beyond merely signifying someone distant
become imbued with that someone's presence.
May each reading this
reach for a needle to knit such a name
to feel someone's presence. 2/23/24

Objects too can carry presence.

While Physically He May be in Texas

If you have an object
so imbued with another's presence
that every time you see it
or hold it in your hand
(like the pen writing these words
thoughtful gift from my son),
then you have what T. S. Eliot
called an objective correlative
reminding me this moment
that while physically he's in Texas
thanks to this pen
my son's heart's in my hand. 2/23/24

Old friends—don't these two words sing off the page?

Had Jesus Gotten to be an Old Guy

What is it with these old guys
carrying on so with their stories
both earnest and whimsical,
pleased to be still hanging together?
You'd think they were little kids.
Jesus never got to be an old guy
but guaranteed he and his pals looking back
would have become again like little children
carrying on with stories earnest and whimsical,
pleased as punch with each new chance
(you never know, possibly the last time)
just to hang together. 2/23/24

This might have been my father's poem had he been a poet.

Stay True to Your Word

Whatever you do
stay true to your word,
or when failing ask forgiveness,
then resolve to do better. 2/23/24

Just one of the gems brought back from Hawaii.

Deep in the Heart Grotto

Lono is the goddess of forgiveness
in whose honor on the Big Island of Hawaii
is set apart a place of refuge
where all no matter their transgression
can come to find refuge.
Raised Catholic I hear an echo
of the Mother of Boundless Mercy.
Imagine Lono and Mary
along with Sophia, Isis, Guan Yin and Gaia
(such astonishing flashing necklace
with separate dazzling gems!)
inviting their children to mercy's sanctuary
deep in the heart grotto. 2/24/24

A follow-up.

Then I Remember Her Name

"I am not worthy" I begin to confess
mindful of my timidity and far worse
but then jolt to remember
that I harbor divinity!
That's precisely why I'm unworthy, I insist,
heedless so often.
Then I remember her name,
Mother of Boundless Mercy. 2/24/24

Perspective alters everything.

Remembering to Say Grace

As I sip orange juice edging toward sour
and eat a banana past ripe,
my mind travels to countless
who would be absolutely thrilled
to have such a fine breakfast.
Then I remember to say grace. 2/24/24

If you're looking for a calling honoring the truth that sets free, journalism sets as high a bar as any.

Glimpses of Hell and Heroism

Watching a harrowing account on Frontline
from the inside of a hospital in Mariupol
of the desperation of doctors and patients
under attack from advancing Russian tanks
thanks to intrepid cameramen
barely escaping with their lives
to bring back footage to counteract lies
threw a whole new light
on war correspondents and heroism. 2/26/24

Bringing "devil" down to Earth.

Father of Lies

If Devil has lost its bite
try Father of Lies.
A case can be made
we have no further to look,
than in the mirror.
Really now, is any of us spotless? 2/25/24

Yet another anniversary.

Beethoven and I can't Forget

I swayed in circles through the house
with a small girl in my arms
to each of Beethoven's symphonies
thirty-eight years ago today.
Of course there were gaps in between
for play and food and nap and such
but always back with her in my arms
for another go-around with Beethoven.
Not yet two she can't remember
but Beethoven and I can't forget. 2/26/24

In 1807 a man smoked a herring—making it red—to distract a nuisance dog. Watch for the distraction in the upcoming race.

Age is a Red Herring

Age is a red herring.
Does it really matter how old
if you are absolutely the best hope
for saving democracy? 2/25/24

Is it not a holy undertaking to listen to another's story?

Invited into a Temple

Listening to another's story
is like being invited into the hush of a temple.
Take off your shoes. 2/27/24

My first counseling position in my new town was at a group home for emotionally disturbed boys—let's just say I was tested.

Something Had to Give

Forty-four years ago today
despite shaking in my boots
I stood my ground against adolescent defiance.
Something had to give
and it wasn't going to be me.
It was not until then that I realized
I had it in me to become a parent. 2/27/24

Proud daddy here.

Scintillating

I remember the best word I could find
to describe the burgeoning spirit
of my daughter when she was a toddler
was scintillating.
I still can't think of a better
as soon she turns 40. 2/27/24

Your life's turning points?
Now there would be a query
to spark deep sharing. 2/28/24

The Windhover by Hopkins will provide context for what follows.

Search for a Metaphor that Catches the Core

Just yesterday a good friend and I—
hurling and gliding down the years
while rebuffing big winds—
realized that of course all along
we'd been falcon brothers!
For any longtime friend,
search for a metaphor
that catches the core. 2/29/24

The Windhover strikes again.

When Poets Soar Grammarians Groan

"My heart in hiding stirred for a bird,
the achieve of, the mastery of the thing!"
Grammarians groan.
What's that supposed to mean, my heart in hiding,
and what's this "achieve of" breaking the rules?
And whoever heard
of a heart stirring for a bird?
Not a poet alive doesn't grasp hearts in hiding
or oblivious to grammar doesn't soar with ecstasy
whenever beholding such high mastery
as the hurl and the gliding
of a Falcon's rebuff of a big wind!
Grammarians looking down can't grasp
what poets looking up can only gasp. 2/29/24

Look around to see where the muzzling is happening today.

Wait! Weren't Others Here First?

The likes of "Promised Land"
and "Manifest Destiny"
succeeded in muzzling conscience
before it could shout out,
"Wait! Weren't others here first?" 2/29/24

Note the reluctance even today to honor the abolitionists.

Abolitionists Seldom Honored

We claim to honor vision and valor
but seldom accord it to the abolitionists.
Ever wonder why? 2/29/24

Call me blessed.

A Wealth of Brothers and Sisters

I have two eagle brothers,
a dragon brother
and a falcon brother.
Add a tree brother,
a brother as enamored of metaphor as I,
another as dedicated to journaling as I,
then destiny brothers from Chicago days
and a brother in beauty
prostrating before snow jewels and periwinkles.
Yes, there was my blood brother,
but I'm talking about something deeper.
As for sisters of my heart and soul,
how would I ever begin? 2/29/24

Can you believe it—
some enamored of Putin
in our very House? 3/1/24

171

This really is a wild ride.

The Whole Shebang Astounds Me

Abiding Presence grounds me,
beauty surrounds me,
evil confounds me,
the whole shebang astounds me. 3/1/24

The lottery's won!
You're alive and you are loved,
now pass the love on. 3/1/2

Don't you love to overhear affection expressed for a valued friend?

Confirmation

To hear his student utter
at mention of his name
"I *love* that man"
heartened me to have confirmed
my own feelings for my friend. 3/1/24

We were made to gawk
so take it slow and easy,
one gawk at a time. 3/2/24

I'm pleased to be one
of those suckers for beauty.
I bet you are too. 3/2/24

Funny the things that stick from a novel read back in high school.

Pondering Love and Death

"What is it makes us love
and makes us die?"
The implication of this plaintive lament
remembered from The Forsyte Saga
is that the utter beauty of the one
is nullified by the abject ugliness of the other.
Yet might part of the reason we love so dearly
be precisely because no life lives forever?
Missing from the equation—
the faith that while every life ends
love lives forever. 3/2/24

Cherish the moment.
When you come right down to it,
what else do we have? 3/2/24

A new meteor—
All the Beauty in the World—
just flashed through my sky. 3/3/24

A new adventure of the universe—is that not each of our days?

The Alchemist will be Surprised Too

Alchemy on my mind,
I'm pondering what ingredients will be added
in this coming day alone
to the concoction in my vessel
guaranteed to make in the universe
a never before seen brew!
To really blow our minds
the Alchemist will be surprised too! 3/4/24

If you're looking for drama.

Meditation Drama

A time to let it settle,
then wait to see what rises.
No judgment,
no coercing,
just fierce attention.
What drama! 3/4/24

What sweet memories
hummingbird when day is done
brings back to his nest. 3/4/24

It's been fifty-one years, but I can still see the shock on their faces.

Exultation and Consternation

I wryly remember it happened on a March 4th,
the day when indeed I marched forth,
boldly declaring to my parents
my departure from the church of my youth
bracing for the ensuing consternation
I knew they would take to their graves. 3/4/24

Nonstop Meditation

I think of meditation
as stepping off the treadmill,
Hummingbird returning to his nest
after humming all day.
"Nonsense," he protests.
"My sweet brand of meditation
is nonstop!" 3/4/24

You don't have to be
an ascetic in a cave
to love the silence. 3/4/24

When you choose to love
imagine a jolt of joy
through the universe.

In response to Patrick Bringley's All the Beauty in the World.

Where Grief Can Take You

⌐⌐

Grief can take you if you let it
to all the beauty in the world
in the museum of your heart. 3/5/24

All our relations—for those close to the Earth, this of course includes the winged ones.

It's Eastern Phoebe I'm Hearing

⌐⌐

Merlin informs me
it's Eastern Phoebe I'm hearing.
How is it not important
when new people enter your life
to learn their names?
Imagine my joy to be learning
the names of each of the members
of the choir in the cathedral! 3/5/24

No wonder he's been so loved down the ages.

Poet of Sky and Earth

⌐⌐

You've missed the heart of St. Francis
if you assume he was speaking metaphorically
when greeting Brother Sun and Sister Moon,
praising Sister Water and Brother Fire. 3/7/24

One of my takeaways from a long ago weekend with Twylah Nitsch, Seneca elder.

When I Begin to Complain about Crow

"Caca weo"—
the simple response to his unmistakable call
was beautiful crow from a revered Medicine woman.
Across decades it comes back
any time I think of complaining
about Crow disturbing the morning. 3/7/24

Think reciprocal welcoming.

Lift Your Heart Sky High

Next time you welcome the sun
lift your heart high as the sky
imagining Sun welcoming you. 3/7/24

I'm reminded of Lincoln's warnings against the ever-lurking "tyrannical principle." Would he now not be cheering Biden?

It will be Thanks to an Intrepid Old Guy

If American democracy survives
after a helluva two-century run
it will be thanks to an intrepid old guy
resolute against yet another eruption
of the tyrannical principle. 3/7/24

In that crafty coot
there's still fire in the belly
and kindness to boot. 3/8/24

Some will understand.

Scoffing will Come from Those Unblessed

Long after I'm gone they still will be here,
these trees surrounding,
and it comforts me to imagine
that deep down they'll remember.
"Pathetic fallacy" comes the scoffing
of those unblessed by long years
lingering with trees. 3/8/24

Consider the possibility that we're less driven by what's behind than lured by what's ahead. Would not the great challenge then be to find the courage to follow the lure?

Coaxed ever Forward

Intuition, intimation, imagination—
see these as future's way
of coaxing us ever forward
just like a dream of an oak
coaxes the acorn awake. 3/8/24

To his daughter late in life: "O, did I ever tell you of a mystical experience I had long ago?"

You will be Safe No Matter What

⌣⟶

"You will be safe no matter what."
That's what he said came to him
whether by actual voice or unquestioned conviction
when as a young man on Lake Michigan
he desperately clung to a boat
in the middle of a savage storm—
not a conviction that he'd be saved
but that he'd be safe no matter what.
I find no better clue
into what sustained Bob Fetter
across a lifetime of sustaining others. 3/10/24

Call me blessed.

Pristine Early Morning

⌣⟶

Dog in my lap,
warmth from the woodstove,
sky outside brightening,
love of my life sleeping—
I have trouble imagining
a way more sweet
a day to greet. 3/9/24

Different dreamer, same dream.

Hold on, Russian Hearts

One day tyranny's tower will topple.
That day Russian hearts
(Navalny's memory sustaining)
will be able to sing with Martin,
Thank God almighty, we are free at last! 3/10/24

An unabashed pitch for progressives.

Before You Knock Progressives

Before you knock progressives
think where every one of your freedoms
would be without them.
Get on board.
Make your life noble. 3/11/24

I bet in your own life this brings someone to mind.

Airy Words Don't Come Close

O I can conjure generosity into airy words
but airy words don't come close
to the generosity Penny breathes. 3/16/24

Reflections upon returning from a trip with the grandkids to Disney World.

Soaring and Sinking Both

Tourist attractions like Disney World
allow us both to soar on wings of amazement
to see marvels of human ingenuity
delighting the child in us all
and to sink almost to despairing
to see the extent of glitter and glut
beyond the reach of literally billions. 3/16/24

Don't you wonder how strict materialists justify their purposeful statements?

Purpose in a Purposeless Universe?

Methinks they have a purpose
in trying to convince the rest of us
that the universe has no purpose.
Of what do they think
they are a living extension? 3/19/24

Solstices get the hoopla, but here's a pitch for equinoxes.

Two Rapturous Equinox Days

Imagine day and night as lovers
twice a year in erotic embrace
birthing Spring in March
then Autumn in September.
Listen and you'll hear Gaia's cry
on these rapturous two days. 3/20/24

Is there any wonder why our ancestors bowed?

Earth's Four Inauguration Days

Solstices sing of dramatic reversals
inaugurating Winter and Summer.
Equinoxes sing of perfect light-dark balance
inaugurating Spring and Autumn!
How not bow with our ancestors
before Earth's four inauguration days? 3/20/24

You say there's no reason to worry?

Rallies across the Country

How the community of culture
in Germany throughout the 1930s
must have trembled when Hitler's rallies
kept crowds whipped to a frenzy. 3/22/24

Without imagination we are imprisoned.

When Is Becomes If

(at the magical hour when is becomes if)—
E. E. Cummings here points
to the power unlocking every door,
opening every window.
Bow when approaching the threshold
of the temple called Imagination. 3/23/24

"Universe" should ignite astonishment.

Universe

Single turning
underscores the elemental connection
of what materialists construe
as a colossal collection of objects,
but what of the live current
of the still-birthing extravaganza
drawing all into the grand sweep
of a colossal communion of subjects?
Feel the pulse.
Creation is unfinished.
We're it! 3/24/24

Check to see how Descartes helped turn anything that couldn't think into a thing.

The Throbbing Universe a Machine?

By ignoring the "within" of things
deemed nonexistent because unmeasurable,
strict materialists smile to imagine
they've dismissed the ghost in the machine.
Really now,
the throbbing universe a machine? 3/24/24

How sad to believe the universe is indifferent.

Put a Smile on the Face of the Universe

If when your head tonight hits the pillow
you have kind actions to look back on,
have you not advanced the very journey
of Great Mystery in love's direction?
Sleep in peace by imagining a smile
on the face of the universe. 3/25/24

The comparison may seem harsh, but can you imagine him holding back on vengeance?

Before Casting Your Vote

Do you really think Trump
would be less savage than Netanyahu
in rooting out what he deemed evil? 3/25/24

Not to see it is to choose not to see it.

No Longer a Speck on the Horizon

Really now, have we ever in our lifetime
valued democracy as we do now?
Chesterton once caught it well:
"The way to love anything
is to realize it might be lost."
The tornado of tyranny
to use Jefferson's stark image
is no longer a speck on the horizon. 3/30/24

Think the gift of each new month!

Imagining Vincent's Excitement

Beginning a new month
is like opening a door
not in fourteen billion years
ever opened before.
Imagine Vincent's excitement
before an empty canvas enticement! 4/1/24

The key is realizing that the universe is not separate, somewhere way out there.

Cutting Edge

To begin to grasp
that the universe is still birthing
and that I'm on the cutting edge
makes the role I have to play today
significant in nothing less
than the rising drama called the universe,
now doesn't it? 4/2/24

Think the odds against any one of us still being here.

Suffused with Awe and Thanksgiving

Without prednisone my lungs
would have succumbed long ago
to recurrences of pneumonia.
In an earlier age pure and simple
I wouldn't still be here.
Just an old guy
suffused with awe and thanksgiving
pondering the mystery of things. 4/2/24

This one brings goosebumps.

No, I will Go Deep in My Hogan

Day of full eclipse—
may holiness not be eclipsed by hoopla.
A Native old one
asked if she's planning to view it
replied "no, I will go deep in my Hogan,
in my heart to hold it." 4/8/24

Either diagnosis accentuates breathing's miracle.

The Preciousness of Breathing

I'm feeling my way, this morning,
into the diagnosis I received yesterday—
asthma instead of pneumonia!
Either way I'm reminded
of the preciousness of breathing! 4/10/24

Once again surprised by joy.

Brown Thrasher's Artistry

Before leaving his perch above me
Brown Thrasher demonstrated the artistry
both of his repertoire and his aim—
splat, right smack on my head!—
to which I exclaimed my acclaim
for such repertoire, such aim! 4/10/24

Before scoffing at Teilhard, allow yourself to be lifted on the wild wings of his truly soaring vision.

Inching the Universe Forward

What if instead of bellowing "Poppycock!"
when hearing Teilhard sing of "amorization"
as the meaning of the forward thrust of the universe,
you pondered with deep satisfaction
as you rest your head on the pillow
after a day of endeavoring to spread kindness
that you had achieved nothing less
than inch the entire universe forward?
Wouldn't you say it beats to hell
the sad vision of seeing yourself
either an inconsequential blip
on a meaningless screen
or else destined to burn for screwing up? 4/10/24

Different instruments to trumpet good news.

Fit as a Fiddle Thanks to the Beat of the Drum

What I heard from my cardiologist today
is that my heart's fit as a fiddle—
my metaphor, not his,
because feeling lyrical at the moment
I'm wondering what music might yet come
thanks to the steady beat of the drum! 4/10/24

Thoughts of mortality might be assumed to depress. Au contraire when I'm reminded of waves of sweetness that keep washing ashore.

Can You Think of a Greater Love Affair?

The day will come when my outgoing breath
will not be met by an incoming.
Weakening lungs provide an educated guess
as to how it will go.
Depressing, you may think, just to think of it?
Actually I'm washed over
by waves of sweetness from the sky ocean
whenever I mindfully breathe it in.
Can you think of a greater love affair
(would you believe across eighty-two years!)
than between lungs and amorous air? 4/12/24

I begin the morning just letting things sink in.

Pondering Immensities

Heavy rain yesterday,
strong wind today.
Morning fire gutters low
as I ponder immensities.
This evening a metallic bird
will fly my Penny home. 4/12/24

April 12th should send shivers down the spine of our memory, reminding of Ft. Sumter.

Before War Decimates

One hundred and sixty-three years ago
euphoria in hearts soared
to hear booms from Charleston Harbor.
Before war decimates
it intoxicates. 4/12/24

Peace Pervades the Morning

A family of deer graze nearby,
check me out and deem me harmless—
must be the pen in my hand,
too small for a gun.
Peace pervades the morning. 4/13/24

Joseph Campbell could not have been clearer with his warning: Beware the error of the found Truth!

Beware the Single Truth

Be slow in presuming
you have found the single Truth.
Why would you then be open
to the truth of another? 4/13/24

Following are several prompted by the eclipse.

The Crescent Sun

I saw it
breaking through the clouds,
the crescent sun!
Totality enough for me. 4/13/24

Moments of Totality

What are we living for
if not moments of totality
not requiring us to cover our eyes? 4/13/24

Praised be Whatever Evokes Awe

Was not feuding forgotten—
between nation and nation,
between science and religion—
when in the moments of witnessing
celestial sun-moon coincidence
we were united in awe?
Praised be whatever evokes awe. 4/13/24

When Darkness Feels Total

When, looking back,
did darkness for you feel total?
End of the world
or prelude to the amazement
of light's eventual return? 4/14/24

There are diehards who still excoriate Lincoln, holding to a mythic lost cause, but thankfully they're in the vast minority. Have we not been given a spirit champion?

A Holy Saturday

It's shortly after 7 on a mid-April morning.
Multiple decades ago at this exact moment
a man's breathing was becoming shallower,
bullet in his brain.
Hushed were the stricken around him
and then his breathing ceased
at precisely twenty-two minutes after seven.
"He belongs now to the ages." 4/15/24

Bird lovers will understand.

Welcoming Back a Presence

When a more than passing acquaintance returns
having been away for months,
how is a cheer not in order?
Welcome back, Thrush, I've missed you! 4/15/24

If the pronoun jolts, consider it a reminder of the hitherto gargantuan imbalance. After all, isn't it a mother who gives birth?

Plug into the Current

When God dreamed up the universe
she decided to incarnate it,
and then there was light
from a blast no ears could hear
spreading creation across eons
to the present flaming moment.
Plug into the Current,
birth something today! 4/15/24

Come listen in The Sea and the Skylark to the poet himself pouring and pelting his music.

Till None's to Spill nor Spend

"And pour and pelt music, till none's to spill nor
      spend"—
may Hopkins' words about the skylark
be true of us each
with nothing left to spill or spend
when reaching our end. 4/15/24

Beauty of course vanishes, but that doesn't lead poets to despair.

Yonder, Yonder, Yonder

"Yonder, yonder, yonder"—
that's where he assures us beauty is kept
with "fonder a care kept than we could have kept it"
while to the forlorn it's sorrowfully clear
beauty is "undone, done with, soon done with."
Lovers of beauty, fearing its ultimate demise,
might check out The Leaden Echo and the Golden Echo
by poet-priest Gerard Manley Hopkins
containing his preposterous claim
that beauty is *not* done with!
O these poets, will ever they face the reality
that beauty is not kept somewhere yonder? 4/16/24

The "totality" keeps coming back.

Are We not All Immersed in It?

All is awash with presence
in these woods surrounding me.
The totality—
are we not all immersed in it,
upheld in mysterious brother and sisterhood
with the standing trees? 4/16/24

If you're looking for good news.

Fulfilling the Primordial Dream

If nothing to us
is more important than love,
good guess to God too—
what else the meaning
of "in the image and likeness"?
Explode with realization amounting to revelation
that each time you're courageous enough to love,
in that precise instant you are in actuality
fulfilling the primordial dream! 4/17/24

Do you have a better guess as to what was behind their singing?

Light, O it's Coming, the Light!

The two loudest voices
in the choir this morning
are Tufted Titmouse and Eastern Phoebe.
I imagine them singing,
"Light, O it's coming, the light!" 4/17/24

Reflecting on the vast difference between wishing and yearning?

Conjecturing on Whence Comes the Yearning

Yearning, yearning, yearning—
of *course* it's so strong
coming from Great Mystery! 4/17/24

Ever imagined God laughing?

They'll have to Beat it with a Stick

"His heart is so strong that after he dies
they'll have to beat it with a stick!"
If I can imagine Jesus laughing,
why not God too? 4/17/24

I keep coming back to this. Can you blame me?

How Not be Astounded?

Never has it happened before
in the whole sweep of the universe
(we're talking nearly fourteen billion years!)
what you can make happen today.
How not be astounded
with this awesome realization
when your feet hit the floor? 4/17/24

The following lines are from "Spring" by Gerard Manley Hopkins.

Rush of Sweetness

Why do I thrill so
to hear Thrush in the distance?
"Thrush through the echoing timber
does so rinse and wring the ear
it strikes like lightnings to hear him sing."
What a rush of sweetness
knowing Hopkins thrilled before me
(I choose to believe thrills with me still). 4/17/24

Thank you Nikki Giovanni. You gave voice when it was needed!

We are Virginia Tech!

"We are Virginia Tech!"
Has a poet ever more captured the moment
thrilling hearts grieving
with pride and resolution?
Seventeen years ago today
but never will we forget it. 4/17/24

Hafiz cut to the chase.

Come Dance with Me

"Come dance with me."
Wouldn't you leap from your seat
to receive such an invitation
each morning from Great Mystery? 4/17/24

Ancestry champions blood, lineage spirit.

Am I not One of Their Offspring?

Hold off pitying
many of my wisdom figures who died childless.
Am I not one of their offspring,
along with countless? 4/18/24

I love touting a book with substance.

Surprise may be Your Reaction

Let Karen Armstrong in her <u>Sacred Nature</u>
open you to the profound respect for the natural world
of each of the world's great religions.
Surprise may be your reaction
to learn Judaism and Christianity
fare least well when compared with the others. 4/18/24

I like imagining Mary Oliver glowing.

Wild Geese in the Distance

What is it about
the sight and haunting sound
of wild geese in the distance
that seizes soul as well as catches breath? 4/18/24

Something to consider next time you're having an identity crisis.

Put that in Your Identity Pipe

Each of us not only reenacts
but advances uniquely
the journey of the very cosmos!
Put that in your identity pipe
and smoke it. 4/18/24

It's always a joy to welcome new members of the congregation.

Welcome Feathered Wayfarers

Pine Siskin and Black-Throated Green Warbler—
welcome, feathered wayfarers, with such captivating
    names
to a choir of distinction. 4/18/24

Did you ever think God too might be on a vision quest?

Reimagining Why We're here

Think of being enlisted by the very universe
in the greatest vision quest of all.
How's that for reimagining
the reason we're here? 4/18/24

Some words are incandescent.

Grace

Some call it sanctifying,
others amazing,
me I call it love
hoping to enlist each of us
in creating a new tomorrow. 4/19/24

Is anything more hopeful than mutual kindness?

Hope in a Time of Peril

The reciprocal kindness today
experienced in exchanges with an auto mechanic
(arms covered with tattoos
including the Confederate battle flag)
speaks hope in a time of peril.
Should we ever meet contesting
political views likely at polar opposites,
I trust it would be respectful
thanks to today's reciprocal kindness. 4/18/24

A laugh early in the morning.

35 Today!

When I came in from my circle of stones
announcing to Penny "35 today!"
she panicked when remembering
we hadn't brought in the plants
and now to learn they came close to freezing!
Imagine her relief when she learned
what I meant was 35 birds! 4/19/24

It would give me great pleasure if you came to see.

Glimpse into My Holy of Holies

Shelf after shelf
reveal treasures in my Cave:
Teilhard de Chardin
Abraham Lincoln,
Frederick Douglass,
Joseph Campbell
Thomas Merton
Gerard Manley Hopkins
E. E. Cummings,
Howard Thurman
Mary Oliver
Carl Jung
Alan Watts
Hermann Hesse
Frederick Beuchner
May Sarton
Loren Eiseley
John Steinbeck
John O'Donohue,
John Yungblut
Thomas Berry
Brian Swimme
Maya Angelou
Thomas Moore,
Sue Monk Kidd.
Pardon the name-dropping
but how else give you a glimpse
into my Holy of Holies? 4/19/24

What is rarer than one of a kind?

Rare Birds

Today was the first visitation
of Gray-hooded Attila—
what a name!
Rare bird for sure,
but then are we not each? 4/20/24

*Check out two poems by Hopkins, "The Sea and the Skylark" and
"Spring," for the the allusions.*

What Music He Pours and Pelts

Tufted Titmouse—
for a little guy
what music he pours and pelts
rinsing and wringing the ear,
hearing him sing strikes like lightnings!
Hopkins sings from the wings. 4/20/24

I mean what am I here for if not to listen?

Message to Their Unfeathered Brother

When I begin to complain that the birds
are distracting me from serious business,
they seem to chastise me in unison,
"Right now, unfeathered brother,
we are your serious business!" 4/20/24

Hmm, would this have brought a shudder to Buddha and Jesus?

I Cheer Today Congress

Despite strong pacifist leanings,
I cheer today Congress
for deciding to fund Ukraine
lest it literally be ground under. 4/20/24

A poet here gets to the heart of it.

I Am!

"for any ruffian of the sky
your kingbird doesn't give a damn
his royal warcry is I AM."
Is not Cummings' kingbird a stand-in
for each of the ten thousand things
not excluding Jesus with his bent
to cry out I AM? 4/20/24

In time of darkness
the thing we can always do:
ourself be a light! 4/20/24

It would seem to be self-evident.

Could a Party Deserve More to be Defeated?

A Putin wing in the House—
can you believe it?—
and led by a once President
refusing to accept defeat,
instead trying by force
to overturn an election!
Could a Party deserve more
to be defeated in '24? 4/20/24

Maybe Merlin was pulling my leg.

Get These Names!

New members of the choir
all making their first appearance:
Golden-crowned Warbler,
Acadian Flycatcher,
Nashville Warbler,
Pygmy Cupwing,
Gray-hooded Attila!
No surprise, it was Earth Day! 4/20/24

I wonder if they drew lots for the colors.

Vireos Returning in Full Color

Having wintered elsewhere
four vireos all returned this morning—
Red-eyed, Yellow-throated, Blue-headed and White-eyed!
I don't buy it was a coincidence.
More likely the Council of the Vireos
summoned them on Earth Day
to delight the surrounding woods and my heart. 4/20/24

Brother deeper than blood Gary Kirby, this one's for you. The dragonfly reference is found in Hopkins' kingfisher sonnet.

Dragonfly Brothers

Brothered by beauty from early Jesuit days,
how interlocked have been their dragonfly journeys—
drawing flame with voice and pen
to their endlessly enticing mistress.
Not till they die will they stop singing,
these devotees to Beauty,
and neither is convinced
they'll even stop then. 4/20/24

Doesn't it deep down ignite something, the very word audacious?

Isn't it Time to be Audacious?

O you of little faith in the cosmos
scheming beyond your wildest dreaming,
isn't it time to follow its lead
and be audacious! 4/20/24

"Quantum field"—fecundity with an aim!

How Does it not Entrance?

There could be no universe
without time intertwined with space.
And can you really call it an "it"
if it has blossomed into the likes of us?
How does it not entrance,
this space-time stupendous dance? 4/21/24

Watch out world, here comes my granddaughter!

Snap, Crackle, and Pop-o-Pop!

Mari's great idea:
a new breakfast sensation for her Pop Pop—
snap,
crackle,
and pop-o-pop! 4/22/24

An alternative to the materialist vision.

Putting Kindness into Context

Don't you wonder if God
ever had any regrets for her dream
(given how mindblowingly long it would take
and at such enormous cost
to so many of her dearly beloved children)
to blossom some day the entire universe into love?
Consider your each act of kindness today
an advancement of her dream! 4/21/24

An invitation for all lovers to look back.

A Month of All Months

November of '75
was the month of all months
in Penny's and my courtship.
You whose courtship
proved foundational for all that has followed,
was there a month of all months
that for you was foundational? 4/22/24

Is not creativity what it's all about?

Helping to Create the Future

The universe has been at it for eons
to reach you and me
with no less a call
than to help create nothing less
than the future!
Wildly grandiose?
Then what do you make
of the universe's long march?
Willy-nilly going nowhere but extinction?
Really? 4/22/24

Numbers aren't what it's about.

Leaving a Vast Feeling

A friend's full-souled response to my poems
calls to mind Steinbeck while writing East of Eden
saying he didn't mind if it were read little
as long as it left a vast feeling.
Deep is my joy
to hear my friend say that my poems
leave in him a vast feeling. 4/23/24

Ah, to know there'll be no clouds tonight to block the full moon!

Anticipating being Entranced

I tingle in anticipation of being entranced
by tonight's full moon.
You who are spirit kin
tingle to understand. 4/23/24

*I used to smile to hear birders waxing lyrical. Chalk it up to
ignorance.*

That Lift at the End of His Trill

Wood Thrush has been holding forth
for over an hour!
You who know the lilt
of that lift at the end of his trill
know well my thrill! 4/23/24

Such company!

Dawn Sounds

I can't tell you how sweet
are Wood Thrush and Tufted Titmouse
harmonizing together
as they herald the sun's coming
from the limbs of standing presences
themselves waving new leaves
in the soft morning breeze. 4/24/24

I think it was Chesterton who said, "The most uncomfortable moment for an atheist is when he feels grateful but has no one to thank."

Joy Magnified

Is not joy magnified
when hearts soaring with gratitude
have Someone to thank? 4/24/24

Ah, how to resurrect the urgent necessity of prayer?

Coming up for Air

Think of prayer
as coming up for air.
It's that vital! 4/24/24

May "the sound of music" call forth lyricism for forest no less than mountain.

Thanks to the Feathered Choir

Alive with the sound of music
thanks to the colorfully-feathered choir
is the towering green cathedral! 4/24/24

Driven by the past or lured by the future—what a difference!

Feel the Lure

Falling in love
or coaxed by love—

prepositions make a difference.
Think love as less present than future
with designs on you from the cosmos!
Sink into silence,
feel the lure. 4/25/24

The play's not only not over, it's our moment on the stage!

Something Dramatic is Afoot

If we're here by blind chance,
by ironclad necessity were all the facts known—
specks willy-nilly blown by a helter-skelter chance
       wind—
I say how then account
for the great love in our hearts?
How can something dramatic not be afoot
in a universe still birthing
calling us each by name to catch fire,
add a unique note to the cosmic choir? 4/25/24

Please don't philosophize (even worse preach) when another is in pain.

Let Them Instead Feel Your Empathy

I'll grant attachment
only magnifies suffering,
but please don't tell those suffering
it's all an illusion.
Let them instead feel your empathy,
the arms of your compassion. 4/25/24

Regarding what to do with beauty, check out "The Leaden Echo and the Golden Echo" by Gerard Manley Hopkins.

Tucked Away in the Sanctuary

What do I do with all this beauty?
I tuck it away in the sanctuary
of God's heart and my own
where candles keep vigil. 4/25/24

Doesn't it bother anyone else?

Capitalize Earth Too!

One of my pet peeves
is when I see Earth uncapitalized.
I mean if Mars and Venus get caps
and Jupiter and Saturn and every other sib,
why not the third planet out
our very Mother? 4/27/24

Does not the shoe fit?

Vice Squad of the Demagogue

Vindictive,
vengeful,
vitriolic,
vicious,
vituperative,
venomous—
think of these v's as the vice squad
at the beck and call of the demagogue
intent (to hell with democracy!)
on raw power.
Please, America, for your future's sake
don't add victorious to the list. 4/27/24

Consider the possibility that love is the end-point of the cosmos,
called Omega by one who could see far.

Before Badmouthing the Universe

Before badmouthing the universe,
take a deep breath
and remember whence love has sprung
and whither it just might be tending. 4/27/24

It takes disciplined endeavor to prepare the soil in every garden.

A Gardening Question

What is your manner
of rock removal and weed-control
in your spiritual garden? 4/27/24

Continuing the same theme.

Be Cultivating Your Heart

Hearts hollowed of love
are ripe for hate.
If to save the world
begin close to home.
Be cultivating your heart. 4/27/24

Rue not your "detours"
seeming to take you off course.
Think what they taught you! 4/29/24

"Everything is grist for the mill" as wise ones used to say.

Everything is Grist

When we catch ourselves ruing
the numerous times in the past
when, headstrong or unready,
we veered far off course,
may we smile to remember
the invaluable things learned
during those times "off course."
Could it be that there's *no* off course,
that everything is grist
for the mill of our journey? 4/29/24

Virgil's lacrimae rerum (the tears of things) invites us to wonder why we don't tear up more.

Seeing a Grown Man Tear Up

Yesterday I had the privilege
of seeing a grown man tear up.
How wonderful that his heart
hasn't kept pace with his body,
has refused to grow old. 4/29/24

"Creation-centered" calls to mind Thomas Berry, Matt Fox and Brian Swimme, all indebted to Teilhard.

Hold on to Your Seats, Spirit Fans

Creation-centered,
meaning centered in the drama of ongoing creation—
what if this were your guiding star,
not what happened long ago
with big bang or fiat lux
but what's happening still now?
Think live current,
wave carrying each forward
including your contribution this very day
to the thrust of the cosmos! 4/30/24

Consider this for a month-ending ritual.

On the Last Day of the Month

On the last day of a month
in gratitude look back on the magnitude
of kindnesses given and received,
challenges faced,
lessons learned.
Then be astounded to realize
that despite your undeserving
with tomorrow begins another! 4/30/24

At least he doesn't pound on his pulpit.

Red-eyed Vireo is Back!

Long months missing his sermons
I thrill to hear the Rev has returned
to climb back into his pulpit
and preach to those of us blessed
to pray in his congregation. 4/30/24

Few birds are so commanding of both visage and voice.

Pileated Woodpecker
has a song like no other,
but then don't we each? 4/30/24

"Make thy claim of wages a zero then, thou hast the world at thy feet." This from Thomas Carlyle gives clue into the requisite attitude for finding the kingdom.

The Wonder and the Joy of It

What did we do to deserve
birdsong this morning,
breath in our lungs?
Nothing, of course—
isn't that the wonder
and the joy of it? 4/30/24

"Privileged" is a cliché word, unless it strikes home.

Imagining into the Lot of the Poor

Primary care physician,
dentist,
optometrist,
audiologist,
cardiologist,
pulmonologist,
dermatologist,
prostate specialist—
all of these I gratefully can afford
but what would happen, I get to thinking,
if like millions (likely billions) in the world
I could afford none? 4/30/24

I choose not to believe in an indifferent God.

God Sick at Heart

Whatever you call this monstrosity,
call it not a just war.
Do any of us escape
having blood on our hands?
I imagine God, sick at heart, weeping—
if not then why call her Love? 4/30/24

Condemning Netanyahu keeps us righteous.

Complicit in the Carnage

How are we who are supplying the arms
not complicit in the carnage? 4/30/24

Two takes on the campus protests.

Parents Agonizing

I'm thinking of parents agonizing
to learn their son or daughter
has abandoned all reason
to protest America's contribution to a slaughter—
"how could they throw away
their education and their future
not to mention our good name?"
I'm thinking of parents agonizing
huddled with their terrified children in Gaza
clinging to a shred of hope that they haven't been
        forgotten
thanks to protests across campuses in America.
"Blessings on those students
risking their education to call attention!" 5/1/24

"Answering" gives the clue.

Answering

⌒

Listening to birds answer each other
calls to mind George Fox
walking cheerfully over the world
answering God in all he meets. 5/1/24

Here I go touting another book.

Sacred Nature

⌒

When seized by a book I must shout it.
Thanks to the amazing scholarship
and deep heart of Karen Armstrong,
our minds are widened and deepened
to see through the lens of each world religion
how the numinosity of sacred nature
lies at its core.
And for an added treat on Audible,
you get to hear her own voice! 5/1/24

The flaw is in thinking the universe is out there.

Hardly Small Potatoes

⌒

You'd think in significance we're infinitesimal,
the smallest of potatoes in the Milky Way's bin,
but how are we not,
when singing out in wonder and thanksgiving,
the Milky Way's own voice? 5/2/24

Could there be a sweeter way to greet May?

May Day Gifts Each One

Sharp cries above me—
Red-shouldered Hawk!
Red-eyed Vireo in the distance
softer but no less insistent.
And then Wood Thrush—
what lilting upswing at the end!
May Day gifts each one
along with standing trees
and rising sun. 5/1/24

Frost's poem is iconic for ringing true whenever we look back on past crossroads, or face new ones.

A Choice in a Yellow Wood

Forty-four years ago today
I passed my oral comps in Richmond—
heretofore teacher
I now was a licensed counselor!
Just an old guy looking back
on a choice in a yellow wood long ago
that made all the difference. 5/2/24

Birds can take you places.

Holy Communion

Eastern Wood-Pewee
has the sweetest way of wishing me good morning.
Suddenly I'm back at Mass
after receiving Holy Communion. 5/2/24

Cutting to the bone.

Find Your Bone

Find your bone! thundered Thoreau.
What I take him to mean
is we're not here to do it all
but to do one thing with all our heart
or else be haunted by something missing
until we find it. 5/3/24

Now really, can anything match early May?

May's Eye-popping Beauty

Multiple-hued iris are peaking,
peonies shout pink, white and red,
ajuga sprawls blue beneath the maple,
climbing roses blaze crimson
while poppies scream orange to the sun—
how futile are words to catch
May's eye-popping beauty! 5/3/24

For all my other pets I have either a burial spot or ashes, for Dromia I have the entire woods.

Surrounding Woods Holy

The last time I saw Dromia,
gray tabby dear to my heart,
was 28 years ago today.
Never finding his body
made the surrounding woods holy.
Not a cat lover alive
who doesn't understand. 5/3/24

Beginning with my 30s, a mandala enshrines each decade.

Mandalas Serving Memory

Within a large circle on a poster board
divided into ten segments
I've begun to fill in the core happenings
across my seventh decade.
Having begun this ritual at the end of my 30s,
I look forward when I'm finished
to behold five mandalas side by side
displaying events of significance
over my life's last fifty years!
Call it one man's endeavor
to visually track his personal evolution,
and should it serve to sow
a seed of possibility in another,
let me know so I just might include it
in my eighth decade's mandala. 5/6/24

Bedrock experiences are never forgotten.

Whatever Door You Came Through

When receiving my First Holy Communion
seventy-five years ago today
I was indoctrinated into believing
I was tangibly receiving God.
Had it been but an idle doctrine
to be dismissed when outgrown
I wouldn't now be remembering it
as a template for all that's come after.
Whatever door you came through,
bless it if it has quickened in you
a hunger for communion. 5/8/24

Same thing in fewer words.

Don't Knock Indoctrination

Don't knock indoctrination until assessing
how affirming is the doctrine.
It might just have opened a door
into the mystery of things. 5/8/24

I likely never would have begun journaling had I not been in crisis.

Revelatory Crisis Journal

My first journal
begun 55 years ago today
was motivated by sheer necessity
meaning my mind was in such turmoil,
my heart in such churning
I couldn't even escape into reading.
Thank goodness TV at the time wasn't within reach
(these were the seminarian days)
or I would have had an easy means of escape.
So I reached for a pad
and began scribbling down the tumult,
at least I could do that.
It took years to reread it
so raw was the panic near frantic
but what window into my soul at the time.
Two wishes for those reading this.
When all else seems to fail
honor your tumult by writing it down,
and please don't throw it away
when things again brighten.
It too belongs in your holy scriptures
for being nothing short of revelatory
of the courage that has seen you through
your remarkable evolution. 5/9/24

Why here if not to give voice?

Find Your Voice

At the UNC graduation in 2010
what I took away from John Grisham's keynote address
was "Find your voice"—
a commendable message
for those commencing their journey,
for the rest of us too. 5/9/24

If every word was once a poem, according to Emerson, then "uni-
verse" is an epic.

To Think We're Each a Part of That!

"Uni" meaning one,
the noteworthy thing about the universe
is that it's all of a piece.
"Verse" meaning turning
signifies a *moving* piece
beginning with a thrust billions of years back
incredibly still advancing!
To think we're each a part of that!
And if we're learning how to love,
how are we not in effect
the very universe learning how to love?
And can you really call it an it
if it has blossomed into you? 5/10/24

The ultimate question for the poet is does it make you want to sing?

Puzzling over "Non-Dual"

If "non-dual" means undifferentiated singularity,
what happens to evident multiplicity
including the absolute individuality
of each mortal selving thing
crying in the rapturous words of Hopkins,
Crying *what I do is me: for that I came.*
By all means bow with your inner mystic
before the fathomless Non-Dual
losing in the process your delusional separate self,
but don't, in the process, deprive your inner poet
of singing of the fathomless wild splendor
of each splendiferous mortal thing
crying what I do is me, for that I came! 5/10/24

Tingling in Anticipation

Two upcoming events
are guaranteed to feed my soul:
energy of spirit at the NAACP Banquet tonight
and heart remembrance tomorrow
at the memorial service of a beloved Friend.
How not tingle in anticipation
of new revelation? 5/10/24

Merlin expands not only my knowledge but my imagination.

Dynamic Duo

Wood Thrush and Red-eyed Vireo,
flutist and preacher—
I think of them as a dynamic duo
inspiriting the morning congregation. 5/11/24

Is counseling all that different from gardening?

Counselors too Sow Seeds

Were counseling your thing
you'd never know when sowing empathy seeds
which might germinate and grow
(soul soil, too, can be too packed or too rocky
and merciless are ravenous birds)
but out of faith you keep sowing.
Then when out of the blue
you receive heartfelt gratitude
for helping to turn a life around,
well, let's say you feel confirmed
in what you do for a living. 5/11/24

Sometimes when exchanging pleasantries something deeper gets sparked.

My Teasing Became a Bow

Learning he grew up near Cincinnati
I began to tease him for betraying the Reds
by rooting for the Dodgers
until hearing his reason in words that sobered—
"Jackie Robinson."
My teasing became a bow. 5/12/24

When someone attends a memorial service for one never met, there's a reason.

How Could I Not?

How beautiful her response
to my wonderment that she came
to a celebration of the life
of someone she had never met—
"How could I not
knowing his transfiguring effect
on the community I've come to love?"
I smile knowing Bob Fetter would have loved her,
and she him! 5/12/24

It's amusing to see the way bird guidebooks try to describe bird calls.

Meeting Great Crested Flycatcher

"Most easily identified by voice:
listen for loud, rising 'queeEEEP'
and various rolling, burry calls."
Having just heard him
then informed by Merlin his name,
I had to look him up
so distinctive his loud rising queeEEEP.
Pleased to meet you, great crested one,
quite fetching the variety
your rolling burry calls. 5/13/24

Thinking here about my faith community.

Trying to Emulate the Forest

You who are at a place in your journey
where the name for the Divine changes
or is no longer needed,
you will be welcomed.
You who have a name for the Divine
so precious you must sing of it,
you will be welcomed.
Let's just say we try
to emulate the forest
in welcoming all voices. 5/13/24

"For the birds" is actually a compliment.

Making Colorful as well as Musical

Red-eyed, Yellow-throated, and Blue-headed—
three Vireos are making colorful as well as musical
a magnificent May morning. 5/13/24

Forty-nine years ago this very day!

Remembering in Awe a Moment

Had she not let her hair down
and worn that blue dress
and looked straight at me and smiled
during her class presentation,
it absolutely would have been
a whole different life.
I invite readers to join me
in remembering in awe a moment
that changed nothing less than the trajectory
of the rest of their lives! 5/14/24

Should action follow rhetoric, we'd be in for it.

Draconian Measures

Should Trump not only escape prison
but get elected in November,
guaranteed "draconian measures"
will take on new meaning. 5/14/24

Hemingway here nails it.

Depending on What You Do Today

⌐⟶

"Today is only one day in all the days that will ever be,
but what will happen in all the other days that ever come
can depend on what you do today."
Who says we're small potatoes?
is what I hear Hemingway here saying. 5/14/24

Here is a surefire way to stop beating up on yourself.

Create Something New Today

⌐⟶

Best way to stop berating yourself
for deficiencies past counting?
Create something new today
that the universe has never seen,
say a random act of kindness
to someone unsuspecting
who will give you back a smile
that can validate your being. 5/14/24

Cause for a heightened self-appraisal.

Ponder Long Who That Is?

⌐⟶

What would it do for your self-esteem
were you to consider that who you are
is a new venturing of the Yearning
that gave birth to the Big Bang?
Ponder long who that is
staring back in the mirror. 5/15/24

At last I'm ready to begin creating a mandala that will harvest my seventh decade.

The Harvesting of a Decade

Ending a decade marks an opportunity
to mine treasures of the preceding ten years.
Annotated calendars help jog memory
but nothing like a journal.
What you do is draw a large circle
(think pie with ten slices, small circle in the center)
then begin filling in each year's slice
saving till the end a distillation
of the entire decade's essence
in that small central circle.
Granted it's a behemoth undertaking
but imagine the pleasure you'd receive
when standing back to behold a mandala
displaying teachings, challenges and illuminations
of a decade unlike any in your own story
not to mention in the story of the world! 5/15/24

Thoreau would approve of this message.

No Way Alone

Surrounded by rooted people,
listening to winged people,
watching four-leggeds scurry for breakfast—
no way I'm alone
out here in the woods. 5/15/24

What Dungeon Must They Dwell In

What terrible disappointment
must have occurred in the lives
of the hardhearted and the mean-spirited?
How otherwise account
for their lack of elemental compassion?
What dungeon must they dwell in,
wealth and power notwithstanding. 5/16/24

Airport mementos.

Eyes Smiling Back

A day in airports
with all the delays and frustrations—
endless walking, endless waiting—
fondly will be forgotten
except for those passing eyes
pausing long enough to reward me
by smiling back. 5/17/2

Something to help me remember a jewel of a morning.

Sweetest Sounds on a Bright Morning

At my son's new home in Ft. Worth
following a harrowing day in three airports,
I'm letting the dust slowly settle
while pondering my granddaughter's blue eyes
as she and Mockingbird out front
are making the sweetest sounds
on a bright Texas morning. 5/17/24

Mockingbird and I
reach deep into repertoires
of songs remembered. 5/17/24

Sticking with mockingbird.

Lyrical Kinship

I choose not to believe
Mockingbird is mocking when he mimics
but rather keeps dipping into his storehouse
to share with the world melodies
he's heard and must repeat.
May we each smile to savor
a lyrical kinship with Mockingbird. 5/17/24

It was not just Mockingbird but the sun on my shoulders.

Create Something New and Never Die

Sunshine on my shoulders
this early Texas morning
raises John Denver from the dead.
You insist he's been gone 27 years?
How so when I'm remembering a song
he bequeathed to the universe?
Create something new on the face of the Earth
and never die. 5/17/24

It's important to know your gifts.

When it Comes to Matters of the Heart

When it comes to things practical
watch out I'm all thumbs
but when it comes to matters of the heart
I take inspiration from mockingbird
gracing any within earshot with her songs.
Come hear us both sing. 5/18/24

It feels fitting to give Mockingbird and a fledging granddaughter the last word in this collection. Hear them both singing together with Riley's Pop Pop.

As Musical as Mockingbird's

I hear baby sounds as musical as mockingbird's
on this soft Texas morning.
Baby, did I say, how could I?
Riley Helen Finn (if you can believe it)
will tomorrow be one year young
while the joy of again being a Pop Pop
will never grow old. 5/18/24

AFTERWORD

It feels fitting to end these twilight ruminations with a rumination from Loren Eiseley in his own twilight years. He was reminded by plums strewn on the ground of the tree's gesture of love toward the universe by hoarding nothing. This inspired him to do the same with his own "carefully hoarded memories." Let's just say his words have inspired me to do the same, hoping that someone, anyone, might be nourished by my own blue plums on the ground. While Eiseley breathed his last in 1977, for adding to the building up of the universe, never will he die.

> "The plums, like some gift given from no one to no
> one visible, continued to fall about me. I was old now,
> I thought suddenly, glancing at a vein on my hand. I
> would have to hoard what remained of the embers…for
> my own head was growing weary and the smoke from
> the autumn fields seemed to be penetrating my mind.
> I wanted to drop them at last, these carefully hoarded
> memories. I wanted to strew them like the blue plums
> in some gesture of love toward the universe all outward
> on a mat of leaves. Rich, rich and not to be hoarded,
> only to be laid down for someone, anyone…"
> (Loren Eiseley, *The Unexpected Universe*, 231-2)

BIOGRAPHICAL INFORMATION

⌒

Charlie Finn lives with his wife Penny north of Roanoke in Fincastle, Virginia. Both are retired and enjoying their life in the country, which includes tending to woodpile and many gardens. Their love of traveling takes them to visits with their children April and Adam in Tennessee and Texas, as well as to enticing points beyond. While Finn retired in 2015 from a 40-year career in counseling, which followed seven years as a high school English and Humanities teacher, he has not retired from his lifelong love of writing. His published writings included the following:

Circle of Grace: In Praise of Months and Seasons (1995)

Natural Highs: An Invitation to Wonder (1999)

For the Mystically Inclined (2002)

Contemplatively Sweet: Slow-Down Poems to Ponder (2004)

Earthtalks: Conjectures on the Spirit Journey (2004)

The Elixir of Air: Unguessed Gifts of Addiction (2005)

Deep Joy, Steep Challenge: 365 Poems on Parenting (2005)

Earth Brother Jesus: Musings Free of Dogma (2005)

Embraced It Will Serve You: Encounters with Death (2006)

If a Child, Why not a Cosmos? Lovesongs to Earth and Evolution (2006)

Fuel for War: Patriotic Entrancement (2006)

Earth Pleasures: Pets, Plants, Trees, and Rain (2007)

Ithaca is the Journey: A Personal Odyssey (2007)

Steppingstones to the Civil War: Slavery Integral to Each (2008)

Aging Liberal Nostalgic for Vision (2008)

Empathy is the Key: Toward a Civil War Healing (2009)

Gentle Warrior John Yungblut: Guide on the Mystic's Journey (2009)

Full Heart Singing: Letters and Poems to a Girlchild (2009)

The Mastery of the Thing!: Transcendence in Counseling and Sports (2010)

Crafting Soul into Words: A Poet Sings of the Journey (2010)

Please Hear What I'm Not Saying: A Poem's Reach around the World (2011)

Roots and Wings: Gifts from Parents (2012)

John Yungblut: Passing the Mystical Torch (Pendle Hill Pamphlet #417, 2012)

Building a Memory Cathedral: Wisdom Figures (2013)

Building a Memory Cathedral: Years, Decades, Months (2014)

O the Mind, Mind has Mountains: Searching for the Heart of Hopkins (2015)

Mandalas Serving Memory: New Ways to Celebrate Your Life (2016)

New Under the Sun: Fecund 2016 (2016)

Focusing on Just One Gift: One Hundred Selected Poems (2017)

Great Day in the Morning: One Hundred Selected Poems (2018)

Sixty to Sing Of: A Wealth of Guardians (2018)

Winter Offerings: Poetry and Prose Dancing (2019)

Mining for Gold: Climbing Mount Empathy and Reclaiming the Mystical (2020)

Witness to the Unvanquished Human Spirit: Poetry for a Troubled Time (2020)

Who's to Say Every Bush is Not Burning?: Poetry during the Pandemic (2021)

Blue Plums on a Mat of Leaves: Ponderings at Break of Day (2022)

Shimmerings and Stammerings: Twilight Ruminations (2024)

Be Creative and Live Forever: Further Twilight Ruminations (2025)

Information about many of Finn's works can be found on his website, www.poetrybycharlescfinn.com. Inscribed copies can be ordered through him at charles.c.finn@gmail.com.